ISBN: 9781313796859

Published by:
HardPress Publishing
8345 NW 66TH ST #2561
MIAMI FL 33166-2626

Email: info@hardpress.net
Web: http://www.hardpress.net

Cornell University Library

THE GIFT OF

Thomas Frederick Crane,

Professor of the Romance Languages and Literatures.

Cornell University Library
arV14942

The philology of the French language.

3 1924 031 684 438

olin,anx

THE PHILOLOGY

OF THE

FRENCH LANGUAGE.

BY

A. L. MEISSNER, Ph.D.,

PROFESSOR OF MODERN LANGUAGES IN THE QUEEN'S UNIVERSITY, IN IRELAND.

*BEING A NEW AND CORRECTED EDITION OF THE
"PALÆSTRA GALLICA."*

---•---

LIBRAIRIE HACHETTE & CIE.
LONDON: 18, KING WILLIAM STREET, STRAND, W.C
PARIS: 79, BOULEVARD ST. GERMAIN.

1874.

"Ne quis igitur tamquam parva fastidiat grammatices elementa: non quia magnae sit operae, consonantes a vocalibus discernere, ipsasque eas in semivocalium numerum mutarumque partiri; sed quia interiora velut sacri hujus adeuntibus, apparebit multa rerum subtilitas, quae non modo acuere ingenia puerilia, sed exercere altissimam quoque eruditionem ac scientiam possit." QUINCT. *Inst. Orat.* i. 4.

PREFACE TO THE NEW EDITION.

The copyright of this book having passed into other hands, and a fresh issue being determined on, I have gladly seized the opportunity of correcting some typographical errors and inadvertencies. The many favourable notices, both in the English and Continental press, as well as the frequent references made to the book in educational works edited by distinguished teachers, show sufficiently that the book filled up a void, and that its publication has promoted a more scientific and serious study of the French language. Students who have mastered its contents will be sufficiently prepared to enter on the study of the "Chanson de Roland," or, what I should prefer, M. Gaston Paris' edition of the "Vie de Saint Alexis." In the introductions to the various versions of this poem, M. Paris has given a complete history of medial French.

As most students read, and most teachers prepare their pupils, for some examination, I have appended a series of examination-questions, which, I trust, will be found useful by both teacher and learner.

Easter, 1874.

ERRATA.

Page 7 line 17 from the top, erase : écluse, sluice, sohleuse, which are derived from the L.L. exclusa.
Page 20 line 11 from the bottom, read : kephalé, caput, for daktylos, digitus.
Page 27 line 19 from the bottom, read ; hambre for hombre.
Page 32 line 16 from the bottom, read : plaudo for plauda.
Page 34 line 4 from the top, read : pécher, to sin, for pêcher.
Page 44 line 12 from the bottom, erase : *the* before oraculum.
Page 52 line 12 from the bottom, read : pécheur for pêcheur.
Page 52 line 10 from the bottom, erase : déshonneur.
Page .78 line 7 from the top, put in : *aut* before (G. w—alt).
Page 89 line 11 from the bottom, read : (pl.) instead of (sing.)
Page 113 line 19 from the top, after *juxta*, add : *de* (do), à (ad).
Page 114 line 7 from the top, read : puisque for piusque.
Page 115 line 15 from the top, read : momifier for moinifier.
Page 115 line 9 from the bottom, read : constitutionnel for constitutional.

CONTENTS.

	PAGE
PREFACE	v
OF THE ELEMENTS OF THE FRENCH LANGUAGE	1
The Romance Languages	1
Low-Latin	3
German Element	6
General Characteristics of Romance Languages	9
Words of Old and Modern Formation	9
OF THE LANGUE D'OÏL	11
Dialects of the Langue d'Oïl	12

PHONOLOGY   15

PERMUTATION OF CONSONANTS	17
Liquids	17
Dentals	19
Gutturals	22
Labials	26
OF VOWELS	28
DOUBLE FORMS AND HOMONYMS	33

MORPHOLOGY   35

OF THE ARTICLES	35
OF THE SUBSTANTIVES	36
Declension	36
Gender and Derivation	38
Gender determined by Suffixes	39
Change of Gender	40
French Gender of Latin Neuters	41
Double Forms and French Communia	42
Derivation of Substantives from Verbs	44
The Crude Form of the Verb used as a Substantive	46

CONTENTS.

	PAGE
Suffixes of Substantives derived from Verbs	49
Suffixes of Substantives derived from other Substantives	56
Suffixes of Substantives derived from Adjectives	64
Suffixes of Diminutives and Augmentatives	67
OF THE ADJECTIVE	72
Declension and Gender	73
Derivation of Adjectives from Verbs	78
Derivation of Adjectives from Substantives	79
Derivation of Adjectives from Adjectives	81
OF THE NUMERALS	81
OF THE PRONOUNS	82
Personal Pronouns	83
Possessive Pronouns	84
Demonstrative Pronouns	86
Relative and Interrogative Pronouns	87
Indefinite Pronouns	87
OF THE VERB	88
Vowel Conjugation	91
Consonant Conjugation	100
Auxiliary Verbs	104
Derivation of Verbs	107
OF THE ADVERB	111
OF THE PREPOSITION	113
OF THE CONJUNCTION	113
OF COMPOUND WORDS	114

APPENDIX

| SPECIMENS OF OLD FRENCH | 117 |

PALÆSTRA GALLICA.

OF THE
ELEMENTS OF THE FRENCH LANGUAGE.

§ 1. Latin, as an inflected language, may be said to have become unintelligible towards the end of the seventh and the beginning of the eighth century. But although dead as an inflected language, it continued to develope itself wherever the Roman power had penetrated. This further development of Latin was not a mere decomposition and corruption of the classical language, but an organic process, which proceeded according to distinct and fixed laws of language. These changes were intimately connected with, and varied according to the literary, social, and political history of the countries which had been subject to the Roman rule, and in which the Roman language was spoken. A fixed and unchangeable language can be conceived only in a fixed and immovable state of society. In a progressive society language must be likewise progressive.

§ 2. The languages which finally developed themselves from Latin into independent idioms, are:—the Italian, Spanish, Portuguese, the *langue d'Oc* and *langue d'Oïl*, and Modern French. The Wallachian, another Romance language, though important for philological purposes, never rose to the dignity of a literary language. France produced two distinct languages, the *langue d'Oc* in the south, and the *langue d'Oïl* in the north. It is the latter which became the parent of our present French language.

§ 3. Although nothing seems more plain and simple than the statement that the Romance languages are a continuation and development of Latin, nevertheless the fact has been but slowly proved, and at times violently contested. At the revival of Greek literature, the origin of the Romance languages was sought in Greek. In 1554, J. Périon published a work, entitled, *Ioachimi Perionii dialogorum de linguæ Gallicæ origine ejusque cum Græca cognatione, libri quatuor.* He was followed, with great skill and erudition, by Henri Etienne, one of the first scholars of his age, in his *Traicté de la conformité du langage françois avec le grec.* To the utmost absurdity went Guichard and Thomassin, the former in his *Harmonie étymologique des langues,* the latter in his *Glossarium universale hebraicum,* in which not only French, but all modern languages are derived from Hebrew. Duclos and La Ravalière maintained that French is a mixture of Latin and Celtic. Their derivations remind one strongly of Dean Swift's witty tract, 'On the Antiquity of the English Language.'

It is only in the present century that the theory of a steady progress and development of language according to settled laws, has been finally established by the labours of Bopp, Grimm, Diez, Pott, and Dieffenbach, in Germany, and Ampère, Chevallet, Littré, Burguy, and Raynouard, in France.

§ 4. The great mistake made by the early philologists was to derive the Modern Romance languages direct from classical Latin, without allowing any intermediate stages of development. This false position produced manifold errors. To remedy these, Raynouard, the father of Romance philology, assumed the existence of an intermediate language, which he called *la langue romane,* and which he supposed to have been the parent of the various Romance languages. This mistake, ably refuted by Sir George Cornewall Lewis in his essay ' On the Origin of the Romance Languages,' was quite excusable in the time of Raynouard. Nearly all the documents on which we base our present researches were then unpublished, and those published had been mutilated and modernised in their grammatical forms. Copyists and editors proceeded on the notion that these early writers used a language of which neither the grammar nor orthography were settled. Every peculiarity and deviation from the modern idiom were ascribed to the ignorance of the authors, texts were corrected by each editor according to the grammar and spelling of his epoch, and only here and there an antiquated expression was left, like an indelible film on a newly-polished surface. Many of the most important documents, especially in *langue d'Oïl,* we shall probably never see in their original form. Now we know that these peculiarities of spelling and grammar were not accidental, but the result of organic changes. The importance of the old spelling for etymological purposes may be seen by one example. The derivation of *debonnaire* seems at first puzzling; but when we find the word spelled in Provençal *de bon aire*, its origin becomes at once plain.*

In order to ascertain correctly the various intermediate changes of the language, recourse has been had to old charters, contracts and private documents, which it was nobody's interest to transcribe from age to age, or to modernise for the better understanding of a later generation.

These intermediate changes are to be found in the *media et infima Latinitas*, in which we observe not only a great change in the conjugations of verbs, declensions and genders of nouns, the use of prepositions, etc., but also a remarkable change in the vocabulary. Archaic words, which occur only in inscriptions and the oldest Roman authors, or are mentioned by classical writers as *vocabula rustica, sordida, vulgaria*, are found in the ordinary spoken and written language. On the other hand, a great many classical words of daily occurrence disap-

* As a specimen of the manner in which even more recent writers are treated by editors, compare the following passage from Froissart. The mutilated text of Buchon is utterly worthless for philological purposes, whilst Lettenhove's edition of the Vatican MS. presents us with a text in the Picardian dialect, and is evidently more trustworthy.

BUCHON.	VATICAN MS.
Lors se partit des crenaux messire Jean de Vienne et vint au Marchet et fit sonner la cloche pour assembler toutes manières de gens en la halle. Au son de la cloche vinrent hommes et femmes, car moult desiroient a ouir nouvelles, ainsi que gens astreints de famine que plus n'en pouvoient porter. Quand ils furent tous venus et assemblés en la balle, hommes et femmes, messire Jean de Vienne leur demontra moult doucement les paroles toutes telles que cidevant sont recitées et leur dit bien que autrement ne pouvoit estre et eussent sur ce avis et brève reponse. Quand ils ouirent ce rapport ils commencerent tous a crier et a pleurer tellement et si amerement qu'il n'est si dure cœur au monde s'il les eut vus ou ouis eux demener qui n'en eut eu pitié. Et n'eurent pour l'heure pouvoir de reponse ni de parler et mêmement messire Jean de Vienne en avoit telle pitié qu'il lacrymoit moult tendrement.	Lors reparti messires Jehans de Viane des barrieres et vint sus le marchie et fist sonner la cloce pour assembler toutes manieres de gens. Au son de la cloce vinrent ils tous hommes et femmes car moult desiroient a oir nouvel'es, ensi que gens si astrains de famine que plus ne povoint. Quand ils furent tout venu et assemble en la place, messire Jehan de Viane lor remonstra moult doucement les paroles toutes et telles que chydevant sont dittes et reciteés et leur dist bien que aultrement ne pooit estre et euissent sur ce avis et brief consel, car il en convenoit faire reponse. Quand il oirent ce raport ils commenchierent tout a crier et a plorer si tendrement et si amerement que il ne fust si durs cœrs au monde, se il les veist et oist euls demener, qui n'en eust pitié, et n'orent pour l'heure nul pooir de respondre ne de parler et mesmement Jehan de Viane en avoit telle pitié que il en lacrimoit moult tendrement.

Even the ordinary texts of Racine and Corneille cannot be trusted for philological purposes. If we should look for a correct text anywhere, it would be certainly in editions for academical studies. But even such men as Géruzez and Jullien have modernized the texts of Corneille in their editions for the *aspirants au baccalauréat*.

pear from the modern language, and are replaced by new derivatives or importations from the German.

§ 5. The following list comprises both archaic and Low-Latin words, with their corresponding French derivatives. The archaic Latin turns up so frequently as mediæval Latin, that it is difficult to give two separate lists, without introducing, in some cases, the same word into both.

The first column contains the classical equivalents of the Low-Latin words, which former have no etymological connection with the words in either the second or third column:—

Classical Latin.	Archaic, or Low Latin.	French Derivative.
anser	auca	oie
adire	aditare	aller
æternus	æternalis	éternel
baculum	bastones	bâton
discere	apprendere	apprendre
edere	manducare	manger
emere	acceptare	acheter
os	bucca	bouche
equus	caballus	cheval
avis	avicella	oiseau
ensis	spatha	épée
exercitus	armata	armée
humerus	spatula	épaule
iter	viaticum	voyage
lapis	petra	pierre
ludus	jocus	jeu
magnus	grandis	grand
mittere	inviare	envoyer
pulcher, formosus	bellus	beau
pulsare	batuere	battre
prœlium	batualia	bataille
verbum	parabola	parole
vertere	tornare	tourner
felis	catus	chat
caverna	cava	cave
dejicere	dejectare	déjeter
directio	directura	droiture
sermo, colloquium	discursus	discours
duplicare	duplare	doubler
palustris	famicosus	fangeux
tabula plana	planca	planche
prope accedere	propiare, appropiare	approcher
caput	testa	tête
portus	baia	baie
ramus	branca	branche
caminus	caminata (room with a fire-place)	cheminée
via	caminus	chemin
gladiator	campio	champion

Classical Latin.	Archaic, or Low Latin.	French Derivative.
centurio, dux	capitanus	capitaine
quercus	casnus	chêne
res	causa	chose
circumvenire	circare	chercher
collis	collina	colline
consobrinus	cosinus	cousin
consuetudo	costuma	coutume
ignis	focus	feu
fons	fontana	fontaine
thus	incensum	encens
prægnans	incincta (quod est sine cinctu)	enceinte
puer, puella	infans	enfant
iter facere	iterare	errer
mutuo dare	præstare	prêter
pretium ponere	pretiare	priser
grex, turba	troppus	troupe, trop
coccineus	vermiculus	vermeil

§ 6. The process of derivation is not symmetrical; that is, we must not seek a corresponding Latin noun for a French noun, a Latin verb to explain a French verb, and so on. But frequently the Latin etymon must be sought in a different category. Sometimes, indeed, the Latin furnishes us with the corresponding etyma for the roots and derivatives of French words. For instance :—

sensus, *sens*	sensibilis, *sensible*
arma, *armes*	armare, *armer*
circulus, *cercle*	circulare, *circular*
bonus, *bon*	bonitas, *bonté*
plangere, *plaindre*	planctus, *plainte*

But sometimes we find the Latin root reproduced in French without the corresponding derivatives: *cœna, cène; fabula, fable; vorax, vorace*; but the French verbs for *cœnare, fabulari, vorare*, are wanting.

On the other hand, we find in French a corresponding derivative, whilst the Latin root has no representative in French. We have *oiseux* from *otiosus*, *irascible* from *irascibilis*, *belliqueux* from *bellicosus*, *vulgaire* from *vulgaris*, *spectacle* from *spectaculum*, *rustre* from *rusticus*; but *otium, irasci, bellum, vulgus, spectare, rus*, are lost in the modern language.

Frequently we find French words which can be explained only by forming a Latin derivative according to analogy. Thus, *sommeil* is explained by *somnicolus*, *soleil* by *soliculus*, *taureau* by *taurellus*, *vaisseau* by *vasillum*.

But of this expedient we must be very chary. In every case we ought to endeavour to find the intermediate links which connect the modern word with the classical, and to prove its existence; otherwise we shall fall into the common error of the old etymologists of inventing words which never had any existence. Witness this example from Ménage. *Aufaine* (*destrier aufaine*) he derives rightly from the Spanish *alfana*, a horse. But to connect it with the Latin, he invents the following intermediate changes: *equus, equa, eka, aka, haka, faka, facana, fana*, and then, with the Arabic article, *alfana*. Now the word is not to be looked for in Latin at all, but comes direct from the Arabic.

§ 7. The invasion of the Roman empire by Germanic tribes in the fifth century introduced into the Romance languages a large number of German words, many of which are lost in modern German. As the conquering nation, they impressed their stamp especially on the vocabulary of warfare. French was further enriched with Germanic elements by the Norman invasion in the tenth century. Although the Normans soon forgot their own language, and assumed that of the conquered race, they nevertheless deposited in the language sufficient proofs of their Germanic origin, especially in words having reference to naval affairs.

The following is a list of words of German origin, some of which have been introduced at a comparatively recent date. Those which have been taken from the Old German, show their antiquity by their having undergone the phonetic changes according to Grimm's law. For convenience' sake, and to assist the beginner, we give the corresponding Modern German or English word, wherever possible.

guerre, *werra* (O.H.G.)
massacrer, *matsken* (*mätzger*)
flamberge, *flamberg*
guivre, *viper*
lansquenet, *landsknecht*
heraut, *herold*
chaloupe, *sloop*
mât, *mast*
est, *ost*
ouest, *west*
boulevard, *bolwerk*
brèche, *brehka* (O.H.G.)
hampe, *handhabe*
havresac, *habersack*
maréchal,* *marschal*
faide, *fehde*
câpre, *kaper*

nord, *nord*
sud, *süd*
élan, *elenthier*
écrou, *schraube*
écrevisse, *krebs*
gazon, (*waso*, O.H.G.) *rasen*
vague, *woge*
garou, *werwolf*
danser,* *tanzen*
haïr, *hassen*
rôtir, *rösten*
cloche, *glocke*
écharpe, *schärpe*
épeler, *to spell* (Engl.)
étoffe, *stoff*
galoper, *galaufan, laufen*
guêpe, *wespe*

* These O. H. G. words seem to have been received back into Modern German after their passage through French.

GERMAN ELEMENT.

haie, *hag*
hareng, *hering*
jardin, *garten*
mannequin, *männchen*
ouate, *watte*
proue, *prow* (Engl.)
rimer, *reimen*
groseille, *krausbeere*
bosquet, *busch*
guise, *weise*
brun, *braun*
blinder, *blenden*
glisser, *glitschen*
gratter, *kratzen*
étamper, *stampfen*
coussin, *kissen*
écluse, *schleuse* (Engl. *sluice*)
faucon, *falk*

fauteuil, *falt-stuhl**
glapir, *klaffen*
guichet, *wicket* (Engl.)
hallebarde, *hellebarde*
harnais, *harnisch*
maçon, (*stein-*) *metz*
meurtre, *murder* (Engl.)
bédeau, *büttel, pedell*
renard, *reinhart*
sabre, *säbel*
rang,
ranger, } *rang*
arranger,
tarir, *darren, dörren*
trinquer, *trinken*
tomber, *to tumble* (Engl.)
wagon, *wagen*

§ 8. Sometimes the same idea has both a Latin and a German representative:—

German.	Latin.	German.	Latin.
blanc	candide	gripper	voler
bouquin	livre	haine	aversion
bourgeois	citoyen	hameau	village
briser	casser	hardiesse	audace
choisir	élire	haveron	avoine
écrevisse	cancer	hase	lièvre
est	orient	honnir	déshonorer
franc	livre	liste	catalogue
le franc	la livre	marquer	designer
franchise	sincérité	nord	septentrion
frapper	battre	ouest	occident
gaîté	joie	sud	midi

The state of feeling which existed between the German invader and the Celtic aborigines is illustrated by the change of meaning undergone by some German words; as, un pauvre *hère*, faire la *lippe*, *lande* maigre, faire la *moue*, une vieille *rosse*, un vieux *bouquin*.

§ 9. Greek has furnished the French and other Romance tongues with a large number of technical terms, imported by the learned. The Greek settlements in the south of France exerted no perceptible influence on the structure or vocabulary of the language. A greater number of Greek words must have been introduced into French, after passing through Latin

---

* 'Un faudestuel d'or fin aporta une serjant.'—*Gaufrey*, p. 260, ed Guessard.

by the earlier churchmen, notably so *parole* (parabola), and *parler* (parabolare). The following few are generally derived from the Greek :—

aise, αἴσιος
bâton, βαστάζειν
bocal, βαυκάλιον
gobelin, κόβαλος
moquer, μωκᾶν
page (le), παιδίον
boutique, ἀποθήκα
bourse, βύρσα
migraine, ἡμικρανία

caravelle, κάραβος
moustache, μύσταξ
osier, οἶσος
parole, παραβολή
plat, πλατύς
saper, σκάπτειν
serin, σειρήν
étouffer, τύφος

But the affinity of the Greek and French languages does not end here. A large number of the etymologies of Etienne are words common to all Indo-European languages. Only it is wrong to say that such or such a French or Latin word is derived from such or such a Greek word. To this class belong the well-known words expressing relationship, the undeniable identity of which first attracted the attention of linguists, and served as a beacon in further researches. Πατήρ, Skt. *pitar*, Lat. *pater*, Goth. *fadar*; from the Skt. root *pâ*, to feed, to protect. Μήτηρ, Skt. *matar*, Lat. *mater*, Old Germ. *muotar*. Φρατήρ and φράτωρ, Skt. *bhratar*, Lat. *frater*, Goth. *brothar*. To these should be added other words in common use, such as οἶκος, vicus, vicinus, voisin; κύων, canis, chien; λέων, leo, lion; οἶνος, vinum, vin; κέρας, cornu, cervus, cerf. All these strike alike the ear and eye. But it is not safe to infer an identity of origin merely from a similarity of sounds. Nothing but strict attention to the history of language will discover a remnant of δίκη, δείκνυμι in the French word *juge* (*ju-dex*); and nothing but the closest attention to the phonetic laws of language can show us the connection between *fils, femme, fi-lius, fi-lia, fe-mina*, and their mutual relation to the Greek root θα, θη (θῆ-σθαι, to milk; θη-λή, breast; τίτ-θη, nurse; θῆ-λυς, female).

§ 10. In changing a language of inflections (synthetic) into one without inflections (analytic), the Romance languages proceed by precisely the same phonetic laws, but under widely different circumstances. Latin displaces in Spain the Iberic, in France the Celtic. Iberic words pass into the one, and Celtic into the other language, but they do so without affecting in any way the structure of the language.

§ 11. In several characteristic processes all the Romance languages agree. These are :—

1. The loss of cases by the destruction of the Latin declensions. A different form is retained only for the singular and plural.*

2. The introduction of *ille* as definite, and of *unus* as indefinite article.

3. The formation of compound tenses by means of auxiliary verbs.

4. By a last effort the mighty form-spirit of the Latin tongue produces, amidst the decomposition of all inflections, a new inflected tense and mood, viz. the future indicative and conditional, by affixing the auxiliary to the infinitive: *aimer*, *-ai*, *-as*, *-a*, etc. It is impossible to derive these forms, as has been attempted, from the Latin futurum exactum, *amaro*, *-is*, *-it*, a proceeding which violates all phonetic laws. The Provençal definitively proves their true origin by spelling the affix as an independent auxiliary.

5. The separate form for the passive voice is rejected and circumscribed by the auxiliary *être*.

6. The neuter gender is merged mainly in the masculine, and only the masculine and feminine genders are retained.

7. The Latin formation of adverbs is replaced by affixing the noun *ment(-em)* to the feminine form of the adjective: *sainement, sanamente*, etc.

8. The Latin manner of forming interrogative sentences by means of particles is superseded and simplified by inverting for the purposes of interrogation the order of the verb and pronoun.

9. The Latin feeling for quantity is generally lost, and gives way to the accent. The syllable which in Latin has the tonic accent, receives the accent in the Romance words. In the present state of the language the tonic accent is a sure guide in distinguishing between words of an earlier and later formation. From the Latin *fragilis* we have in French both *frêle* and *fragile*. The former retains the accent on the same syllable as the Latin word, besides undergoing the vowel-change. This is conclusive proof of the antiquity of the word. *Fragile*, on the other hand, moves the accent to the affix and retains the Latin vowel, which proves that the word was formed directly from the Latin, at a later time, not by the people but by the race of bookmen. Other examples are:—

Latin.	Old Formation.	Modern Form.
acceptare	acheter	accépter
blasphemare	blâmer	blasphémer

* Of the old French declensions, and the retention of a distinct form for the accusative, we shall speak hereafter.

Latin	Old Formation.	Modern Form.
calculus	caillou	calcul
campus	{ champ / champagne	camp / campagne
canalis	chenean, chenal	canal
cantor	chantre	chanteur
capitulum	chapitre	capitule
captivus	chétif	captif
caput	chef	cap
casa	chez	case
catena	chaîne	cadène
causa	chose	cause
charta	charte	carte
costuma	coutume	costume
decimare	dîmer	décimer
divinus	devin	divin
ducatus	duché	ducat
examen	essaim	examen
factio	façon	faction
gravis	grief	grave
hospitalis	hôtel	hôpital
implicare	employer	impliquer
Isara	Oise	Isère
ligare	lier	liguer
major	maire, majeur	major
ministerium	métier	ministère
modulari	mouler	modeler
monasterium	moustier	monastère
nativus	naïf	natif
opera	œuvre	opéra
organum	orgue	organe
parabola	parole	parabole
pastor	pâtre	pasteur
pausare	poser	pauser
pensare	peser	penser
Persica	pêche	persique
pietas	pitié	piété
potio	poison	potion
redemptio	rançon	redemption
rigidus	roide	rigide
Romanus	romain	roman
sacramentum	serment	sacrement
scandalum	esclandre	scandale
securitas	sûreté	sécurité
separare	sevrer	séparer
serviens	sergent	servant
singularis (*sc.* epur)	sanglier	singulier
sollicitare	soucier	solliciter
species	épice	espèce
strictus	étroit	strict
superficies	surface	superficie
vigilia	veille	vigile

10. The preponderating influence of accent over quantity produces in poetry a new metric law. Verses are now composed according to accent, and no longer according to quantity. Hence we speak of Greek and Latin as *quantitative* languages, and of the Romance (as well as the Germanic) as *accentuating* languages.

§ 12. Some of the changes observable in the modern tongue are foreshadowed in vulgar and archaic Latin. So, for instance, it is of importance to us to find Ennius using *pulvis* as a feminine (*la poudre*), and *cupressus* and *laurus* as masculines. We derive additional light from the fact that St. Augustine advised the preacher to say *ossum* instead of *os*, so that he might be better understood by the common people. From the former example we learn that the gender of the spoken and not of the written language was received into the modern tongue; from the latter we infer that the common people had probably a simplified declension of nouns.

OF THE LANGUE D'OÏL.

§ 13. Two distinct languages developed themselves in France out of the Latin. In the south, the langue d'Oc or Provençal, and in the north the langue d'Oïl. It was the latter which, through the political preponderance of the people, became the universal tongue of the inhabitants of France. In comparing both the langue d'Oc and langue d'Oïl with the other Romance tongues, we observe as the most striking characteristic that they still have a remnant of declensions. They retain a separate form for the nominative (*cas sujet*) and for the accusative (*cas régime*). The two cases assume an identical form only in the fifteenth century, from which time, accordingly, we may date the origin of the Modern French language.

§ 14. It is a strange and inexplicable fact that the languages which were the first to accomplish a decomposition of the Latin, were not the first to develope a literature. Dante flourished in the fourteenth century. But the troubadours of Provence, and the trouvères of the north, had long before that produced a rich literature, although the grammatical state of the language was not so far advanced as that of Italian. For no one would think at the present day of speaking of the langue d'Oc and langue d'Oïl as mere patois, in which a number of local poets wrote. They were the literary and polite languages of their time, and were learned and used as media of literary composition by foreigners. Children were sent to France to learn the langue d'Oïl, and Richard Cœur de Lion wrote verses in Provençal.

§ 15. The langue d'Oïl, according to Burguy, Fallot, &c., has three principal dialects, which coincide with the three great political centres, and are called after them, *Bourguignon*, *Normand*, and *Picard*. To these Littré adds a fourth, which he calls *la langue du Centre*, and of which others have spoken as *le dialect Français*, or *le dialect de l'Isle de France*. This dialect, however, is at present scarcely distinguishable from the Burgundian dialect.

These three dialects have the same grammar, but differ in some peculiarities, especially in the vowels, so as to be easily distinguishable one from another. All the three dialects have contributed towards the formation of modern French. Thus we have from the Burgundian *pois* (*poids*), and from the Norman *peser*; from the Burgundian *roy*, and from the Norman *reyne*; *attacher* from the Burgundian, and *attaquer* from the Picardian. The subjoined table represents the most common differences and interchanges of vowels in the three dialects:—

Normandy.	Picardy.	Burgundy.
e	oi, ai, ie	oi, ai, ei, ie
ei	oi, ai	oi, ei, ai
u	o, on, eu	o
ui	i, oi, oui	ui, oi, eui, oui

For example:—

Latin.	Norman.	Picardian.	Burgundian.
rex	rei	roi	roi
te	tei	toi, ti	—
bonus	buen, buene	boin, boune	boin, boine
pavor	poür	paour	peor
flos	flur	flour	flor
habere	aveir	avoir	—
cadere	cheir	queir	chaoir, chaire
sapere	saver	sçavoir	savoir
piscis	peissuns	poissons	peissons
quid	qnei	quoi	quoi
sit	seit	soit	—
sint	seient	soient	—
manducare	manger	mangier	mengier
color	culur	colour	—

§ 16. The Norman dialect has the following peculiarities:
1. It rejects the *i* of most words ending in *ie, ier, ai, air,* is, *derrere, lesser, plerc.*

2. The simple letter *u* is used instead of *o, ou, u, eu, oi* and sometimes even for *a*. This frequent use of *u* is continued for a long time, especially in Anglo-Norman, and has appeared to some a mark of great antiquity, which is far from being the case.

3. The final *t* is replaced by *d*. *Fud* instead of *fut*.

4. The nasal sounds are weaker, or disappear entirely.

5. *Ei* is always substituted for *oi*, particularly in the terminations of the imperfect: *diseit, penseit, feseit,* instead of the Burgundian or Picardian *disoit, pensoit, fesoit*. The Burgundian dialect, long after it had accepted the Norman pronunciation of this termination, still retained its own peculiar spelling. The dialect of Picardy has retained its old pronunciation.

The dialect of Picardy shows a predilection for *ch*, hard *c* or *k*, and final *g*. For instance: *canchon, ichi, chiel, kanoine* or *canoine, commenchier*, for *chanson, ici, ciel, chanoine, commencer*.

6. The *o* and *a* of the Burgundian dialect are changed into *e*.

The Burgundian dialect is chiefly marked by the addition of an *i* (*diphthongaison*) to *a* whether in the beginning, the middle, or at the end of a word, and to the *é fermé pur*. Thus, *demandei* for *demandé, gouverneir* for *gouverner, li peire* for *le père, lai* for *la, tai* for *ta, teils* for *tels, asseiz* for *assez, acheteir* for *acheter*.

Another peculiarity of the Burgundian dialect is the use of *g* for expressing the nasal sound: *juig* for *juin*.

PRONUNCIATION OF THE LANGUE D'OÏL.

§ 17. To fix the pronunciation of a dead language is a matter of great difficulty. The orthography of the langue d'Oïl has a far closer resemblance to the orthography of the Latin language, from which fact we may safely infer that its pronunciation was likewise more like the Latin. Any change in the spelling of a written language presupposes, however, a long established change in the pronunciation. For this reason it has become customary to pronounce old French words like their representatives in modern French. Some differences of spelling seem to be merely graphic, and no indications of a difference in pronunciation. Thus the sound represented at present by *eu* was frequently represented by *ue*, as *puet* for *peut, cuer* for *cœur, ues* for *œufs*. Old French *x* is frequently equivalent to *ux* : *yex* for *yeux*, *chevax* for *chevaux*, *beax* for *beaux*. The phonetic change of *l* into *u* is not expressed in writing till a late period. Thus we have *altre* for *autre*, *halt* for *haut*. Before the invention of the circumflex accent, various means were adopted for expressing long vowels. The most usual were the doubling of the vowel, or the addition of an *e* or *i*. Thus we read *aage*, *aige* and *eage* for *âge*, *meur* for *mûr*, *blesseure* for *blessure*, *que je feisse* for *fisse*.

PHONOLOGY.

§ 18. THE PHONOLOGY of the French language is one of the most difficult tasks of the comparative grammar of the Romance languages. Italian has preserved the sounds of classical Latin most faithfully; next in order come Spanish and Portuguese, whilst French sounds deviate more than those of any other Romance tongue from those of Latin. Sounds and phonetic changes occur in French, which are not to be found in the cognate languages. On the other hand, a more accurate study of French sounds as compared with archaic Latin and Umbrian, is destined, no doubt, to throw considerable light on the history of the Latin language. We can point out only a few important points.

§ 19. The final *s m t* and particularly the final *nt*, which are so important in the inflection of nouns and verbs, are sometimes expressed in writing in archaic Latin and Umbrian, and sometimes not. From this we may infer, that these letters, if pronounced at all, were so but slightly. In fact, we may suspect that the inflectional terminations were beginning to wear off, that a decomposition had begun, which was arrested by the sudden rise of Latin literature. In the written language these final letters became fixed, but in the vulgar tongue the decomposition went on. *Amaverunt* vel *amavere*, *fuerunt* vel *fuere*, is learned at present by every school-boy in his primer. That final *nt* has retained its place in the orthography of the French language till the present day: *aimèrent, furent*. When the orthography of a language has once been fixed, any subsequent changes in pronunciation, even after they have obtained currency amongst the educated, are but slowly received into the written language.

§ 20. Another remarkable case is the history of the aspirate. In all European languages the *h* has gradually lost its harsh sound, and the process of weakening is still at work. The Italians write it in a few instances, but never pronounce it. The same is the case with the modern Greek spiritus asper. In Latin the aspirate appears originally in combination with labials and dentals: *bh, th, gh, ch, dh, th*. Gradually either the aspirate or the mute proves the stronger and displaces the other. Thus the Umbrian has the aspirate only before *t*, and this *h* or *ch* becomes in Latin *c* : *uhtur, auctor*; *frehtu, frictum*; *rehte, recte*. Frequently the Latin *h* seems to have been a modification of the Italic *f*, a sound peculiar to the Italic dialects : *harena* is found by the side of the Sabinian *fasena*; Latin *hircus, ircus* answer to to the Sabinian *fircus*. And within the circle of Latin itself we have *hœdus* and *fœdus*, *hebris* and *febris*, *horreum* and *farreum*.

As regards the pronunciation of *h* in the classical period, the Romans seem to have been very much in the same position as we at the present day in England. 'Rusticus fit sermo si aspires perperam,' says the grammarian Nigidius Figulus (apud Gell. xiii. 6, 3), from which it appears that uneducated people used the aspirate in the wrong place. Instructive is the following passage from Quinctilian: 'Apud nos potest quæri, an in scripto sit vitium, si *h* litera non est notata? cujus quidem ratio mutata cum temporibus est sæpius. Parcissime ea veteres usi etiam in vocalibus, cum *œdos ircosque* dicebant. Diu deinde servatum, ne consonantibus adspiraretur, ut in *Graccis* et *triumpis*. Erupit brevi tempore nimius usus ut *choronæ, chenturiones, præchones* adhuc quibusdam inscriptionibus maneant : qua de re Catulli nobile epigramma est.' (Lib. i. cap. v.) Even the best Roman grammarians differ as to the aspirate. In French, the number of words in which the *h* is aspirated, and in which it is always initial, has dwindled down to less than three hundred words.

§ 21. Another highly important change in the form of French words can be carried back to a very high antiquity. The shortening of the final syllables, which has resulted in the final mute *e* of the French, began probably before the golden age of Latin literature. Many final vowels are found long in the old poets, which are used as short by the classical poets. Thus Ennius says :—

> Et densis aquilā pennis obnixa volabat;

where the final *a* of the nom. *aquila* is used as long. The same poet says :—

> Multa foro ponit et ageā longa repletur;

where the nom. *agea* is used with the same quantity.

§ 22. The study of languages leads us here to the same results as the study of the physical sciences. We find the human mind inclined to underrate the age of things as soon as some very limited period, easily grasped by the common mind, is exceeded. Our men of science fix the date of the creation of the world and of man at a period far more remote than was generally accepted but a short time ago. In the same way, to understand aright the origin and formation of the Romance languages, we must go back not merely to the Media and Infima Latinitas, but still further to the earliest records of Italic dialects, and even to the prehistoric age of the Latin language. The Romance languages are not divided from their Roman prototype by a period of barbarism, and a stage of confusion of languages, as was formerly supposed. There is one steady organic process. Such forms as *pelegrinus, quattro, congiunta,* which are found in the oldest epigraphic monuments, are rather Romance than Latin, and exhibit phonetic changes characteristic of the languages of the present day.

OF CONSONANTS.

§ 23. The consonants are, to use an old simile, the bones of a language, and serve the same purpose in philology as the skeleton in comparative anatomy. In considering their phonetic changes, we shall find that their position in the word is of the highest importance. Double consonants and consonants in the beginning of a word have a greater resisting power than consonants in the middle or at the end of a word. We therefore shall frequently consider the same consonant under three different aspects; as initial, in the middle (medial??), or final.

I. The Liquids.

§ 24. The liquids have retained in French their original Latin form more frequently than the mutes. They are chiefly subject to (a) interchangeability, especially *l* with *r* and *r* with *l*; (b) transposition, and (c) the change of the semivowel *l* into the vowel *u*.

L instead of *r*: flairer, *fragrare*; autel, *altare*.

R instead of *l*: rossignol, *lusciniolus*; grimper, *klimban* (O.H.G.); orme, *ulmus*; chapitre, *capitulum*; apôtre, *apostolus*; épître, *epistola*; titre, *titulus*; chartre, M. L. *cartula*; esclandre, *scandalum*.

The interchange between *l* and *r* is very old, especially the softening of the hard *r* into *l*. This was called τραυλισμός or *balbe loqui*. Compare also, λείριον, *lilium*; ἀστήρ, *stella*; βάρβαρος, *balbus*.

R instead of *n*: diacre, *diaconus*; timbre, *tympanum*; ordre, *ordinem*; Londres, *Londinium*.

N instead of *m*: nèfle, *mespilum*; nappe, *mappa*; contèr, *computare*; printemps, *primum tempus*; rançon, *redemptionem*; ronger, *rumigare*; singe, *simius*; songe, *somnium*; vendange, *vindemia*; congé, *commeatus*.

M instead of *n*: homme, *homin-em*; femme, *femin-am*; nommer, *nomin-are*. This change occurs only in the middle of a word. Final *m* especially is liable to change into *n*: ton, *tuum*; mon, *meum*; son, *suum*; rien, *rem*.

U instead of *l*: du, *de illo, del*; au, *ad illum, al*; poudre, *pulverem*; chevaucher, *cavalcare*; haut, *altus*; chaud, *calidus*. Words from the German follow this analogy: Guillaume, *Willehalm*; Thibaut, *Theobald*; heaume, *helm*; heauberc, *halsberc*.

Metathesis of *l* and *r*: pour, *pro*; trouble, *turbidus*; flûte, *fistula*; goupil, *vulpes*.

At and near Paris it is very common to say *berloque* instead of *breloque*. Spiers gives both forms, without marking either as a vulgarism. Chevallet calls the latter a vulgarism, and classes it with *ferlaté* for *frelaté*, *brélue* for *berlue*, *bertelle* for *bretelle*, *fremer* for *fermer*, *breline* for *berline*. From *adbibere* is formed at first *abevrer*, *abeuvrer*, and then by transposition, *abreuver*. From the noun *bord* two verbs are formed: *border*, and, with a different meaning, by transposition, *broder*.

The intercalation of *b* and *d* between two liquids is a euphonic change peculiar to French amongst the Romance languages:—

Cendre, *cinerem*; gendre, *generem*; moindre, *minorem*; poudre, *pulverem*; tendre, *tenerem*; pondre, *ponere*; vendredi, *Veneris dies*. And with the rejection of *g*: ceindre, *cingere*; feindre, *fingere*; peindre, *pingere*. This phonetic change is however known to Greek (ἀνήρ, ἀνδρός) and to German (*Fähndrich*).

Marbre, *marmor*; chambre, *camera*; nombre, *numerum*; concombre, *cucumerem*; foudre, *fulmen*; combler, *cumulare*; humble, *humilis*; sembler, *simulare*; trembler, *tremulare*; moudre, *molere*. Intercalated *d* is likewise found in the futures *voudrai, viendrai, faudra, vaudrai, tiendrai*.

MUTES.

§ 25. The mutes present to us the most characteristic phonetic law of the Romance languages. In the beginning of a word they remain generally unchanged, but in the middle of a word the tenuis is changed into the media, and the media frequently into a vowel: *t* becomes *d*, *c* changes into *g*, *p* into *b*, *d* falls away, *g* is vocalised into *i*, and *b* into *v* (*u*.)

The aspirates are unknown to the Latin and to the Romance languages. Their *th*, *ph*, and *ch* are merely orthographic varieties of the corresponding tenues, and mark generally the Greek or Old High German origin of the word; as, *théologie, mathématique, Théodore, Thibaut.*

This change of the tenuis into the media is, as has been observed, the characteristic law of the Romance languages. The great phonetic law of the Germanic languages (which is the change of media into tenuis, and of tenuis into aspirate), forms a direct contrast to it.

Dentals (t, d, z, s).

§ 26. Initial *t* remains unchanged with the exception of donc, *tunc*; and craindre, *tremere*. The latter change is an anomaly, only the inverse of it is found in the O. F. veintre, *vincere*.

In the middle of a word *t* is changed into *d*, or suffers syncope. The latter case is the most frequent: coude, *cubitus*; fade, *fatuus*; Adour, *Aturis*; saluer, *salutare*; chaire, *cathedra*; chaîne, *catena*.

The change of *t* into the sibilant, whether expressed by *s* or by *t*, is confined to words derived from Latin compounds with the suffix *ti*. This suffix serves in Latin for the formation of abstracta from verbal roots; as, *men-ti, par-ti, ar-ti, mor-ti*, many of which are enlarged by the suffix *on*: *men-ti-o, por-ti-o, na-ti-o*. This *t* before *i*, with following vowel, was assibilated even in the golden age of Roman literature, and in the Low Latin passed into the sound of *z*. The change into *s* is also orthographically expressed in raison, *rationem*; poison, *potionem*; chanson, *cantionem*; tison, *titionem*; Venise, *Venetia*; and in deriv. adj. oiseux, *otiosus*. In a few instances a *ss* is found: justesse, *justitia*; paresse, *pigritia*. Assibilated *t* is the rule in almost all other cases: nation, portion, patience, notion, fraction.

Final *t* remains (graphic) in monosyllables, but disappears in polysyllables: tout, *totus*; lit, *lectus*; fut, *fuit*; vertu, *virtutem*. Gré, *gratus*, and salut, *salutem*, are exceptions. In the terminations *at-em, ut-em* (with the exception of *salut*), the tenuis disappears regularly, and so in the participial terminations, *atum, itum*: duché, *ducatus*; abbé, *abbatus*; cité, *civi-*

tatem; vérité, *veritatem*; aigu, *acutus*; chanté, *cantatum*; donné, *donatum*; fini, *finitum*; rendu, *redditum*; but the *t* is preserved in Old French in the part. perf. of the 2nd and 4th conjugations: *sentit, renduit.*

In the combination of *tr*, the *t* always suffers syncope: père, *patrem*; pierre, *petra*; frère, *fratrem*; nourrir, *nutrire*; pourrir, *putrire*; verre, *vitrum*; errer, *iterare*.

Words of modern formation preserve a graphic *t* at the end of the word: *ingrat, légat, délicat* (but O. F. *delié*), *mandat, crédit, débit, dévot, institut, appétit.*

Extraordinary is the change of *t* into *f*: *soif*, sitim.

D.

Initial *d* remains unchanged: dire, *dicere*; deux, *duo*. In the middle of a word syncope takes place most frequently: ouïr, *audire*; hui, *hodie*; sueur, *sudor*; envie, *invidia*; choir, *cadere*; clore, *claudere*; moëlle, *medulla*; rançon, *redemptionem*; envahir, *invadere*. At the end of a word *d* is either thrown off, or remains a mere graphic *d*: à, *ad*; nœud, *nodus*; cru, *crudus*; foi, *fid-em*; froid, *frigid-us*; chaud, *calid-us*; pied, *ped-em*; rond, *rotundus*; Arnauld, *Arnaldus*.

Assimilation takes place in arrière, *adretro*; lierre, *hedera*.

In the middle of a word *d* frequently maintains itself, especially in words of modern formation: *odeur, nudité, rude*; and also between *n* and *r*: fendre, *findere*; vendre, *vendere*; and before following *r*: Adrien, *Hadrianus*; Adriatique, *Adriaticum*; édredon, (Germ.) *eiderdown*.

In the combination *dr* (cf. *tr*) syncope takes place regularly: rire, *ridere*; croire, *credere*; voir, *videre*; louer, *laudare*; confier, *confidere*.

Irregular is the change of *d* into *l*: cigale, *cicada*. Compare δάκρυ, lacryma; δάκτυλ-ος, digit-us.

In Latin compounds, we have *t* with following *r* softened into *d*: *quadraginta, quadringenti, quadratus, quadragiens.*

Z (ds).

The *z* of modern French, at the beginning or in the middle of a word, has its origin chiefly in a Greek ξ: zone, zéphire. The final *z* is traceable to a Latin *s*: nez, *nasus*; chez, *casa*; rez, *rasus*; assez, *satis*: avez, *habetis*; vendiez, *vendebatis*. In Old French *z* was used as an inflectional letter, taking the place of the modern *s*: granz, citéz, coronéz, venduz, cumandemenz; and also sanz, *sine*; souz, *subtus*; enz, *intus*.

DENTALS. 21

From a Latin c in the middle of a word we have : onze, *undecim*; quinze, *quindecim*; seize, *sedecim*; lézard, *lacerta*. Gazon is from O. H. G. *waso*; zero from Arab. *cifron*.

S.

Latin *s* is generally represented in French by *s*, and has apparently undergone more changes in pronunciation than in spelling, especially between two vowels in the middle of a word. A few cases occur of the interchange of *s* and *r*, so common in Greek: *vaslet* and *varlet*, *chaise* and *chaire*. Compare παῖς, *puer*.

When *s* and *r* come together, in consequence of the syncope of a vowel or Latin *c*, *t* is intercalated between *s* and *r*: connaître (O. F. conostre), *cognoscere*; paître (O. F. paîstre), *pascere*.

Of frequent occurrence is the syncope of *s* in modern French, where Old French has retained the sibilant: être, estre, *stare*; âne, asne, *asinus*; île, isle, *insula*; âpre, aspre, *asper*; pâtre, paistre, *pastorem*; chacun, chascun, *quisque unus*; carême, caresme, *quadragesima*. This *s* is frequently retained in proper names: *Dufresne, Lestoile, Le Forest, Levesque*.

Compare with this the following Latin formations: *jūdex* (jus-dex), *ĭdem* (ĭs-dem), *pōno* (pŏs-no), *corpulentus* (corpus-lentus), and forms like *tra-duco, tra-do*, with those of *trans-duco, trans-do*.

The combinations *sp, sc, st*, so frequent in Latin, are softened in the Western languages by prefixing an *e*. It seems that the Celtic nations were unable to pronounce an initial *s* before a consonant, or at least that they disliked it. The Spaniards in Peru, even when reading Latin, pronounce *estudium* for *studium*, *eschola* for *schola*; and in Latin inscriptions of the fourth century after Christ we find *ispiritus, istatua*. But even nations who had not the faintest difficulty in pronouncing an initial *s impurum* have a tendency to prefix a euphonic vowel, so that we may here have to do rather with a general *musical law* of language than with any peculiarity of the Celtic languages. Thus, in Greek we have: ἀσκαίρω = σκαίρω, ἀσπαίρω = σπαίρω, ἀσπάλαξ = σπάλαξ, ἀσπαρίζω = σπαρίζω, ἀσταλύζω = σταλύζω, ἄσταχυς = στάχυς, ἀσταφίς = σταφίς, ἀστεροπή = στεροπή. Compare also ἀστήρ with L. *stella*, and ὀδούς with L. *dens* (dent-s), Skt. *dant*, and ἀνήρ with Skt. *nar*. In French we find many examples: espérer, *sperare*; espèce, *species*; esprit, *spiritus*; espace, *spatium*; escalier, *scala*; esclandre, *scandalum*; escabeau, *scabellum*; estomac, *sto-*

machus. At a later period this *s* is frequently thrown off, but the *e* retained with an acute accent: épais, *spissus*; épi, spica; épaule, *spatula*; établir, *stabilire*; étain, *stannum*; état, *status*; étoile, *stella*; étude, *studium*. Words of German origin follow this rule: épervier, *sperber*; éperon, E. *spur*; escrime, G. *schirmen*; étuve, E. *stove*. In words of modern formation we have *sp, sc, st* also in the beginning of French words: *spirituel, spécial, statue, scribe, sculpteur, stabilité*, and even in the ' Cantilène de Ste. Eulalie' we read *une spede.* The *sc* of *sçavoir* and *scierge* in Old French are mere whims of orthography.

In Latin a similar phonetic law is observed with respect to initial *sn, sm, sr*. Wherever these consonants stood in the beginning of a word, the *s* is thrown off: *nix*, originally *snig-s* (compare G. *Schnee*); *nurus*, originally *snurus* (comp. G. *Schnur*).

GUTTURALS (k [c, q], g, j, h, i).

§ 27. The *k* sound is most frequently expressed in Latin by *c* or *q*. This guttural sound in the beginning or middle of a word is softened into *g*, or suffers syncope: gras, *crassus*; gobelet, *cupella*; gonfler, *conflare*; figue, *ficus*; aigu, *acutus*; cigale, *cicada*; église, *ecclesia*; aigle, *aquila*; égal, *æqualis*. And from the G. grimper, *klimmen* (O. H. G. *klimban*); gratter, *kratzen* (O. H. G. *chrazôn*). An apparent exception is *second*, the *c* of which, however, is pronounced like *g*. The Burgundian dialect has *segont*.

Final *c*, with few exceptions, is thrown off: feu, *foc-us*; lieu, *loc-us*. Lac, *lacus*, and estomac, *stomachus*, preserve a graphic *c*.

Very old and difficult of explanation is the change of initial *c* before Latin *a* into *ch*. Its origin is lost in the remotest antiquity, and is anterior to any written documents of the language. Diez has ascribed it to Frankish influence; but the opinion of Burguy, that it is owing to Celtic influence, receives confirmation from the prevalence of *ch* and *k* in the dialect of Picardy: chaîne, *catena*; chair, *caro*; chambre, *camera*; cheveu, *capillus*; chenu, *canutus*; chaleur, *calor*; chef, *caput*; chèvre, *capra*; chien, *canis*; échelle, *scala*; chou, *caulis*; chose, *causa*. In the middle of a word: coucher, *collocare*; sécher, *siccare*; fourche, *furca*; marchand, *mercantem*; lache, *laxus*; lacher, *laxare*; péché, *peccatum*; bachelier, *baccalarius*; prêcher, *prædicare*; empêcher, *im-*

pédicare; arracher, *eradicare*; nicher, *nidificare*; mâcher, *masticare*; fléchir, *flectere*; bouehe, *bucca*. The exceptions are remnants of old dialects which did not admit the *ch*: caisse, *capsa*; campagne, *campania* (but also *Champagne*).

C before *e, i, y, œ, æ*, changes into a lingual and has a sound approaching *s*. In Latin every *c* appears to have had originally the sound of *k*. Many documents of the sixth and seventh centuries have been preserved in and near Ravenna, in which *c* before *e* and *i* is invariably transliterated by Greek κ: φεκιτ, δεκιμ, πακειφικος. Another proof of the originally guttural sound of *c* is its frequent interchange with *q*. 'Duæ ex his' (sc. mutis), says Maximus Victorinus (Ars Gram. 18), 'supervacuæ videntur *k* et *q*, quia *c* litera eorum locum possit explere.' The change of pronunciation took place probably in the seventh century.

C before *e* and *i* changes into *s*: gésir, *jacere*; voisin, *vicinus*; plaisir, *placere*; loisir, *licere*; oiseau, *avicellus*; disais, *dicebam*. And also at the end of a word: fois, *vic-em*; souris, *soric-em*; brebis, *vervec-em*.

In the middle of a word syncope of *c* frequently takes place before *e* or *i*: faire, *facere*; plaire, *placere*; taire, *tacere*; dire, *dicere*; reduire, *reducere*; luire, *lucere*; nuir, *nocere*; exploit, *explicitum*; grêle, *gracilis*; and before *a* in louer (to let), *locare*.

C before *t* is frequently assimilated, but syncope takes place quite as frequently: jeter, *jactare*; lutter, *luctari*; lutrin, M. L. *lectrum*; étroit, *strictus*; droit, *directus*; nuit, *noctem*; contrat, *contractum*; effet, *effectum*; joint, *junctum*; conduit, *conductum*; peint, *pictum*; saint, *sanctum*. The original *c* frequently remains: as, *acteur, docteur, octobre, affliction*; and in avec, *apud hoc*.

In the combinations *dc, nc, rc, tc*, the *c* is generally changed into *g*, whilst *d* and *t* are thrown out: sauvage, *silvaticus*; voyage, *viaticum*; juger, *judicare*; manger, *manducare*; venger, *vindicare*; clergé, *clericatus*.

Compare: κυβερνήτης, gubernator; εἴκοσι, viginti.

Q.

Q is in most cases only an orthographic variety of *k*, and retains generally this sound: quel, *qualis*; qualité, *qualitas*; cadre, *quadrum*; car, *quare*; casser, *quassare*; comme, *quomodo*.

In a few words the *u* after *q* is sounded: *aquatique, aquarelle, équateur, quadragénaire, quadragésime, quadrangulaire, quadrature, quadrisyllabe, quadrilatère, quadrupède, quadruple, loquace, quartz, liquéfaction, questeur, questure, équestre, équitation, requiem, équilatéral,* and a few others.

The tenuis changes into media in égal, *æqualis*; and syncope takes place in Seine, *Sequana*; eau (O. F. aive, eve), *aqua*.

G.

The media *g* had in the Romance languages much the same fate as the tenuis *k*. Its change depended on the following letter. In French, *g* remains in the beginning of words, but has become very rare in the middle: roide, *rigidus*; froid, *frigidus*; lire, *legere*; reine, *regina*; châtier, *castigare*; géant, *gigant-em*; lier, *ligare*; nier, *negare*; noir, *niger*; païen, *paganus*; pèlerin, *peregrinus*; plaie, *plaga*; royal, *regalis*; août, *augustus*; paresse, *pigritia*; entier, *integer*; bonheur, *bonum augurium*; malheur, *malum augurium*;* faine, *fagina*; maître, *magister*; frêle, *fragilis*; trente, *triginta*. A graphic *g* remains in doigt, *digitus*.

Latin *g* before *a* becomes *j*: joie, *gaudium*; jouir, *gaudere*.

More firmness is shown by the combination *gn*: digne, règne, signe.

Of peculiar interest is the Latin combination *ng*, in which *g* is thrown out, and a *d* intercalated: ceindre, *cingere*; feindre, *fingere*; peindre, *pingere*; plaindre, *plangere*; éteindre, *extinguere*; teindre, *tingere*; astreindre, restreindre, *restringere*; enfreindre, *infringere*. The intercalated *d* of the infinitive and future of these verbs is thrown out in the present and imperative, whilst the original Latin form reappears in the imperfect and preterite.

The syncope of the gutturals *c* and *g* after *r* and *l* with a following *t* or *s* is a general phonetic law of the Latin language: *sar-tus (sarc-io, sarc-tus)*; *tor-tus (torqu-eo, torc-tus)*; *ul-tor (ulc-isci, ulc-tus)*; *in-dul-tus (in-dulg-eo, in-dulc-tus)*; *sar-si (sarc-io, sarc-tus)*; *tor-si (torqu-eo, torc-si)*; *spar-si (sparg-o, sparg-si)*; *quin-tus (quinque, quinc-tus)*. At the end of a word, however, *rcs* occurs; as, *arx, merx*.

* The popular derivation from *hora* is contradicted by the gender, the termination, and the meaning. The simple *heur*, properly *eur*, occurs frequently in Corneille (Cinna v. 1; Cid iii. 4). The O. F. *aür* is always used as a dissyllable. The *h* owes its origin to a mistaken notion as to its etymology. The contraction of *augurium* into *heur* has nothing surprising. Compare L. or-aculum = augur-aculum, and E. Austin = Augustin.

J.

This letter, which in Latin had neither the sound of a vowel nor of a consonant, assumes in French the form of a consonant, which process, according to Maximus Victorinus (Ars Gram. 18), had begun in Latin: '*i* et *u* loco consonantum etiam ponuntur, quando aut ipsæ inter se geminantur, aut cum aliis vocalibus junguntur, veluti si sit in capite *v*: vorsus, virus, volvitur:' juge, *judex*; jeune, *juvenis*.

In a few instances, however, *j* becomes a vowel: aider, *adjutare*; maire, *major*; raie, *raja*.

H.

The peculiar sound of the Latin *h*, which was originally not a mere aspirate, but an aspirated labial, accounts for some phonetic changes in the Romance languages. Forms such as *haba* for *faba*, *hordeum* for *fordeum*, *hebris* for *febris*, and *fest-uca* by the side of *hast-a*, show that *h* must, at least in certain words, have had a labial sound. Gradually either the labial prevails over the aspirate, or the reverse. In the latter case the aspirate became gradually weakened, and being capable of but few phonetic changes, was almost entirely lost. This process began in the very earliest times of the Latin language. Thus we have from *homo* both *nemo* (ne-homo) and *femina* (hom-, fom-ina, and with the same vowel-change as in *nemo*, fem-ina). In the case of *nemo*, the aspirate first ejected the labial, but in its turn was lost by its inherent incapacity for phonetic change. In the case of *femina*, on the other hand, the labial sound remained firmly, whilst the aspirate was lost.

In the middle of French words *h* has occasionally retained its force in order to avoid hiatus: *cohorte*, *véhicule*.

In some words initial *h* is onomatopœtic: *hennir*, *hocher*, *haïr*, *haine*, *haro*, *hibou*, *hurler*, *huer*, *hisser*. The German aspirate seems to have resisted better than either the Latin or Greek: *hareng*, *halte*, *hallebarde*, *hardes*, *haubans*, *haubergeon*, *haubert*, *Havre*, *havresac*, *héraut*, *hernutes*, *homard*, *houppelande*, *Henri*, in the last of which the *h* is gradually becoming silent.

Labials (p, b, f [ph], v).

P.

§ 28. *P* initial and *pp* show great firmness. Only in two instances has an initial Latin *p* changed into the media: bruine, *pruina*; bocal, *poculum*.

In the middle of a word *p* changes into *b*, but more frequently into *v*: louve, *lupa*; poivre, *piper*; chevron, *capronem*; chèvre, *capra*; œuvre, *opus*; savoir, *sapere*; sève, *sapa*; recevoir, *recipere*; ouvrir, *aperire*; cuve, *cupa*; cheveu, *capillus*; neveu, *nepotem*; rive, *ripa*; prévôt, *præpositus*; double, *duplus*; abeille, *apicula*; ciboule, *cæpula*; Grenoble, *Gratianopolis*; timbre, *tympanum*.

In words of modern formation, the *p* remains: vapeur, capitaine, peuplier, triple, stupide.

In chef, *caput*, and nèfle, *mespilum* we have examples of the rare change of *p* into *f*.

P before *t* and *d* is frequently thrown out or assimilated: chétif, *captivus*; noces, *nuptiæ*; route, *rupta* (sc. *via*); malade, *male aptus*; recette, *recepta*; grotte, *crypta*; écrit, *scriptum*; manuscrit, *manuscriptum*; tiède, *tepidus*; caisse, châsse, *capsa*. Nevertheless from the fourteenth to the sixteenth century the *p* reappears in a great many words, in some of them merely as a silent letter or with a somewhat subdued sound: prompt, *promptus*; compter, *computare*; baptême, *baptisma*; sept, *septem*.

Final *p* has remained sometimes as a silent, sometimes as an audible letter: exempt, *exemptus*; corps, *corpus*; temps, *tempus*; abrupt, *abruptus*; laps, *lapsus*.

B.

Initial *b* has always remained *b*; but in the middle of a word the change into *v* is observable at an early period. Latin inscriptions have forms such as *incomparavilis*, *acervus*. The change of *b* into *v*, and subsequently into *u*, is especially observable between two vowels with following *r*: ivre, *ebrius*; fève, *faba*; lèvre, *labrum*; livre, *liber* and *libra*; avoir, *habere*; prouver, *probare*; devoir, *debere*; cheval, *caballus*; où, *ubi*; soudain, *subitaneus*; soulever, *sublevare*; ôter, *obstare*; souvenir, *subvenire*; coude, *cubitus*.

But even between two vowels *b* has frequently maintained itself: habit, *habitus*; subit, *subitus*; globe, *globus*; obéir, *obedire*; habile, *habilis*; and in connection with liquids: arbre, *arborem*; arbuste, *arbustum*; albâtre, *alabastrum*;

Ambières, *Ambibari*; diable, *diabolus*; fable, *fabula*; table, *tabula*. Before consonants which begin a new syllable it is likewise maintained frequently: obsèques, *obsequiæ*; obscur, *obscurus*; absence, *absentia*; abdiquer, *abdicare*; abject, *abjectus*; subtil, *subtilis*; obvier, *obviare*.

Final *b* has remained only after nasal sounds: plomb, *plumbum*; Colomb, *Columbus*; rumb, ῥύμβος, ῥόμβος.

Exceptional is the change of *bb* into *m*: Samedi, *Sabbati dies*; and rare the change of *b* into *f*: suif, *sebum*; siffler, *sibilare*.

F (ph)

The peculiar sound of the Latin *f* (*h*), which has been mentioned before, is thus described by Quintilian (Inst. Orat. xii. 10): 'Nam et illa quæ est sexta nostrarum pæne non humana voce, vel omnino non voce potius *inter discrimina dentium efflanda est*; quæ etiam cum vocalem proxima accipit, quassa quodammodo, utique quoties aliquam consonantem frangit, ut in hoc ipso "frangit" multo fit horridior.' And Priscian, speaking of this letter, says (i. 14): 'Hoc tantum scire debemus, quod non fixis labris est pronuntianda *f*, quomodo *ph*, atque hoc solum interest.'

This close resemblance of *h* and *f* is traceable in two French etymologies: habler, *fabulari*; and hormis, *foras missum*. The Spanish furnishes us with the striking change of initial *f* into *h*: hijo, *filius*; hombre, *fames humo*, *fumus*.

The French *ph* is a mere orthographic variety of *f*, and in Old French the latter was constantly substituted for the former, as *fisicien*, etc.; and occasionally *v*, as Steven, *Stephanus*, whence the English form is derived.

V.

In the beginning and in the middle of words original *v* has frequently maintained itself, even between vowels and in connection with *r* and *l*: vain, *vanus*; vin, *vinum*; vivace, *vivacem*; priver, *privare*; grave, *gravis*; cadavre, *cadaver*; vivre, *vivere*; servir, *servire*.

On the other hand, a hardening of Latin *v* into French *b* takes place in the beginning and the middle of some words: brebis, *vervex*; bariolé, *varius*; courbe, *curvus*; corbeau, *corvus*; Besançon, *Vesontion-em*.

Final *v* changes almost always into *f*: bref, *brev-is*; nef, *nav-is*; œuf, *ov-um*; bœuf, *bov-em*; chétif, *captiv-um*; nerf, *nerv-um*; serf, *serv-um*.

The change of *v* into *f* has by some been ascribed to Germanic, by others to Celtic influence : gater, *vastare*; guêpe, *vespa*; gaîne, *vagina*; gui, *viscus*. And from the German : garder, *warten*; gazon, O. H. G. *waso*, M. G. *rasen*; guichet, E. *wicket*; Gauthier, *Walter*.

Syncope of *v* has taken place in : paon, *pavon-em*; peur, *pavor-em*.

OF VOWELS.

§ 29. The vocalism of the French language deviates greatly from that of the Latin language, and cannot be traced to the same fixed laws as the phonetic changes of the consonants. Still, some laws may be observed, especially in the changes of vowels which have the tonic accent, or which are long either by nature or by position. Vowels long by position are said to be long either by original (Latin) position or by Romance position. The former case is regulated by the Latin rules of quantity ; the latter case arises when, by the syncope of a Latin vowel, a new position is produced by the juxtaposition of a mute and a liquid, or of a double consonant, as in *femme*, *fable*, *manche* (manica). Long vowels (like the double consonants) show more firmness than short vowels, favouring thus the assumption that a long vowel is a double short one, that $\bar{a} = \breve{a} + \breve{a}$.

Of all vowels *i* has shown most firmness. Next comes *u*, which is closely related to it; then *a* and *o* : *e* is the most variable of the vowels.

Very frequent in the Romance languages is the modification of the vowel (*diphthongaison*) by the addition of a short *i*, which greatly resembles the German *Umlaut*. This modification of the vowel prevailed especially in the langue d'Oïl : *aige*, *raige*, *caige*, *rochier*, *couchier*, *vergier*; and in Modern French : *plein*, *neige*, *peine*, *treize*.

Of great importance is the law regulating the coalition of vowels, which may be brought about either by the vocalization of a consonant (as *aurai*, *aune*), or by syncope of a consonant (*chaîne*, *catena*, *traître*, *traditorem*). The unaccented vowel, as a rule, is merged in the accented vowel.

§ 30. Subjoined is a tabular view of the most ordinary vowel-changes :—

Latin.	French.
a	a, ai, e
ē	oi, e
ĕ	ie
e long by position	e
ī	i

Latin.	French.
ī	e, oi
i long by position	e
ō	eu, o
ŏ	eu, o
o long by position	o
ū	u
ŭ	o, ou
u long by position	o, ou

DIPHTHONGS

æ	ie, e
œ	e
au	o

A.

§ 31. *A* is preserved in original Latin position: cheval, *caballus*; val, *vallum*; pâle, *pallidus*; haut, *altus*; flamme, *flamma*; an, *annus*; pan, *pannus*; plante, *planta*; char, *carrus*; charme, *carmen*; arbre, *arborem*; gras, *crassus*; vache, *vacca*; âpre, *asper*; art, *artem*.

In Romance position: chambre, *camera*; âme, *anima*; diacre, *diaconus*; âne, *asinus*; voyage, *viaticum*; volage, *volaticus*; sauvage, *silvaticus*; aimable, *amabilis*. Add to these: rage, *rabies* (*rabjes*); cage, *cavea* (*cavja*).

The unaccented *a* of prefixes, such as *ab, abs, ac, ad, apo, anti, af*, is frequently preserved: *abonder, abstraction, abstrait, accéder, accélerer, accent, adapter, adverbe, apologie, apologue, antiphone, antipode, affable, affaire.*

Before *m* and *n*, no other consonant following, *a* changes into *ai*: aime, *amo*; daim, *dama*; faim, *fames*; essaim, *examen*; demain, *mane*; laine, *lana*; sain, *sanus*; vain, *vanus*; romain, *romanus*; chapelain, *capellanus*. The suffix *ien* forms an exception: *chrétien, indien, italien, égyptien, païen.*

Before all other simple consonants, even before *r* (notably so in the infinitives of the first conjugation), *a* changes into *e*: quel, *qualis*; tel, *talis*; sel, *sal*; échelle, *scala*; mortel, *mortalis*; autel, *altare*; amer, *amarus*; cher, *carus*; donner, *donare*; habiter, *habitare*; and into *ai* with syncope of the following consonant: mais, *magis*; faîne, *fagina*; ai, *habeo*; faire, *facere*.

But if *a* has the tonic accent it is preserved before simple consonants: *mal, canal, rare, case, cas, rase, état.*

E.

The changes of Latin *e* in French deviate greatly from those of the other Romance languages. Whilst in the others *ē*, whether long by nature or by Romance position (cf. It. *mese, mensis*), remains, French generally changes it into *oi*: avoine, *avena*; crois, *crēdo*; dois, *dēbeo*; moi, *mē*; toi, *tē*; soi, *sē*; toile, *telum*; étoile, *stella*; trois, *trĕs*; voile, *vĕlum*; avoir, *habēre*; coi, *quiētus*; mois, *mensis*; bourgeois, *burgensis*; poids, *pensum*; toise, *tensa*; loi, *lēgem*; roi, *rēgem*; loyal, *lēgalis*; royal, *rēgalis*; toit, *tectum*; poitrail, *pectorale*; doyen, *dĕcanus*; soixante, *sexaginta*; voiture, *vectura*; espoir, *sperare*.

Nevertheless, the original *e* remains frequently: céder, chandelle, complet, cruel, fidèle, espérer; and before *n*, when it is generally modified by *i*: frein, plein, haleine, veine.

In a few words *e* changes into *ai*: craie, *crēta*; taie, *thēca*; cannaie, *cannetum*; faible, *flebilis*.

E into *i*: cire, *cera*; venin, *venenum*; pris, *prensus*; merci, *mercedem*; pis, *pejus*; brebis, *vervecem*; raisin, *racēmus*; six, *sex*; lit, *lectus*; marquis, *marchensis*.

Short *e* before a simple consonant changes regularly into *ie*: bien, *bĕne*; fièvre, *febris*; lierre, *hedera*; mieux, *melius*; vient, *venit*; tient, *tĕnet*; sied, *sedet*; lièvre, *lĕporem*; entier, *integer*; tiède, *tepidus*; miel, *mel*; hier, *heri*; fier, *ferus*. Sometimes even long *e* undergoes this change: rien, *rēm*; cierge, *cēreus*; ciel, *cœlum*; siége, *sēdes*; but rarely *e* long by position: tiers, *tertius*; biel, *bellus*. *E* in position generally remains *e*: fer, *ferrum*; cent, *centum*; prudent, *prudentem*; terre, *terra*; fenêtre, *fenestra*.

Before *r* and *n*, especially if the vowel has a nasal sound, *e* changes sometimes into *a*: par, *per*; lucarne, *lucerna*; lézard, *lacerta*; séant, *sedendo*, *sedentem*; courant, *currentem*; marchand, *mercantem*.

I.

Long *i* remains unchanged: crime, vivre, figue, fils, livre, admirer, nid, finis, punir, épi (spica), tige (tibia); except in carène, *carina*.

Short *i* = *oi*: boire, *bibere*; foi, *fides*; moins, *minus*; poire, *pirus*; soit, *sit*; roide, *rigidus*; voie, *via*; vois, *vides*; doigt, *digitus*; quoi, *quid*; soif, *sitis*; moindre, *minorem*; poivre, *piper*. And likewise in O.F: *consoilz, mervoille*, which in M.F. follow the second rule.

Short *i* = *ei*: oreille, *auricula*; conseil, *consilium*; neige, *nivem*; feindre, *fingere*; sein, *sinus*; enseigne, *insigne*; corbeille, *corbicula*; merveille, *mirabilia*.

Short *i* = *e*: trèfle, *trifolium*; justesse, *justitia*; veuve, *vidua*; verd, *viridis*; tristesse, *tristitia*; posséder, *possidere*.

Subject to the same laws as short *i* is *i* in position: étroit, *strictus*; but more usually *e* : ferme, *firmus*; sec, *siccus*; en, *inde*; lettre, *littera*; cep, *cippus*; trente, *triginta*; souvent, *subinde*; fendre, *findere*; mettre, *mittere*.

I before original *ng, gn, nc=ei* or *ai* : ceindre, *cingere*; peindre, *pingere*; enseigne, *insignis*; enfreindre, *infringere*; daigner, *dignari*; vaincre, *vincere*.

Peculiar is the change of *i* into *a* : langue, *lingua*; sangle, *cingulum*; dans, *de intus*; sans, *sine*; sanglot, *singultus*.

Vierge from *virgo*, in contradistinction to verge, *virga*.

O.

No distinction is observable in the changes of long *o* and short *o*. The simple vowel is preserved usually only before *m* and *n*. The predominant change is *o=eu* or *œu*.

O=o : couronne, *corona*; nom, *nomen*; personne, *persona*; lion, *leonem*; comme, *quomodo*; pomme, *pomum*; pondre, *ponere*; or, *hora*; Rome, *Roma*; raison, *rationem*.

O=eu, œu : meuble, *mobilis*; mœurs, *mores*; neveu, *nepotem*; nœud, *nodus*; œuf, *ovum*; pleure, *ploro*; seul, *solus*; vœu, *votum*; honneur, *honorem*; glorieux, *gloriosus*; aqueux, *aquosus*; and the rest in *or* and *osus*; leur, *illorum*; jongleur, *joculatorem*; neuf, *novus*; neuf, *novem*; veux, *volo*; meurs, *morior*; feu, *focus*; jeu, *jocus*; jeudi, *Jovis dies*; linceul, *linteolum*; filleul, *filiolus*; cœur, *cor*; œuvre, *opera*; and with the modification of an *i* : œil, *oculus*; cueille, *colligo*; chevreuil, *capreolus*; cercueil, *sarciolus*.

O = ou : nous, *nos*; vous, *vos*; pour, *pro*; époux, *sposus* (*sponsus*); Toulouse, *Tolosa*; proue, *prora*; avoue, *voto*; doue, *doto*; noue, *nodo*; tout, *totus*.

O = ou : roue, *rota*; éprouver, *exprobare*; moulin, *molina*; courage, M. L. *coragium* (*cor*). From *o* in position : tourne, *torno*.

Exceptions : huis, *ostium*; huître, *ostrea*; puis, *post*.

U.

Long *u* remains almost without an exception, but receives the pronunciation peculiar to French *u*. This pronunciation, unknown to the other Romance tongues, seems to have been known to the Romans. Compare such forms as *optumus pessumus, lacruma, existumo*, with the more usual *optimus* etc. Quintilian says (i. 4) : 'Et medius est quidam *v* et *i* literæ sonus. Non enim sic *optimum* dicimus, ut *opimum*.'

Sûr, *securus*; pur, *purus*; cuve, *cupa*; écu, *scutum*; vertu, *virtutem*; nue, *nubes*; un, *unus*; aigu, *acutus*; brume, *bruma*;

confus, *confusus*; exclus, *exclusus*; cru, *crudus*; fus, *fui*; glu, *gluten*; enclume, *incūdem*; jeûne, *jejunium*; juge, *judicem*; Juin, *Junius*; luit, *lucet*; mûr, *maturus*; mur, *murus*; nu, *nudus*; nature, *natura*; menu, *minutus*.

Short $u = o$ before nasal consonants: son, *suum*; ton, *tuum*; mon, *meum*; nombre, *numerus*; and diphthongally with *i*: croix, *crucem*; noix, *nucem*; coin, *cuneus*; point, *punctum*.

Short $u = ou$: coude, *cubitus*; joug, *jugum*; où, *ubi*; doute, *dubito*; souvent, *subinde*; soudain, *subitaneus*.

U in position undergoes the same changes as short *u*; before nasals it changes into *o*, and otherwise into *ou*: ongle, *ungula*; plomb, *plumbum*; dont, *de unde*; flot, *fluctus*; mot, M. L. *muttum*; noces, *nuptiæ*; vergogne, *verecundia*. Double, *duplex*; ours, *ursus*; sourd, *surdus*; sous, *subtus*; tour, *turris*; doux, *dulcis*; foudre, *fulgur*; soufre, *sulphur*; goutte, *gutta*; jour, *diurnum*; souvenir, *subvenire*; cours, *curro*.

German *eu* is in *butin, beute*; and *u* in *cruche, kruog, krug*.

Æ, Œ.

Æ = ie: *ciel, siècle, lié* (lætus).
Æ = e: *grec*.
Æ, Œ = oi: *foin* (fœnum), *proie* (præda).
Œ = e: cénacle, pénal, cénotaphe.

Au.

Latin had the same tendency, observable in French, of shortening diphthongs into monophthongs. This shows itself in such forms as *Claudius, Clodius*; *cauda, coda*; *plauda, plodo*; *lautus, lotus*. The modern languages here continue the process: clore, *claudere*; chose, *causa*; trésor, *thesaurus*; and diphthongally with *i*: joie, *gaudium*; cloître, *claustrum*; oie, *auca*. The etymological spelling of *au* is often retained, though the sound is that of *o*: *pauvre, restaurer, cause, fraude*.

Au = ou: alouette, *alauda*; ou, *aut*; louer, *laudare*.

Paucus makes O. F. *pau, po*, and then *peu*; cauda, *coda, queue*.

Of Unaccented Vowels.

§ 32. Vowels in unaccented syllable seem to have a mere numerical value, and their changes are subject to many accidents.

In an unaccented first syllable *a* is frequently put instead of *e* and *i*: farouche, *ferox*; marché, *mercatus*; paresse, *pigritia*; jaloux, *zelosus*; chacun, *quisque unus*.

Latin vowels which become silent or are subject to excision, are almost always represented by *e* mute : aime, *amo*; âme, *anima*; Virgile, *Vergilius*; Horace, *Horatius*.

DOUBLE FORMS AND HOMONYMS.

§ 33. As one or the other of these phonetic laws came into operation, the modern word assumed a different form. Not to speak of words of modern origin, which are derived direct from Latin, without undergoing any physiological change, we find, that from one and the same Latin word two different modern forms are derived by phonetic laws. Generally speaking, some different meaning attaches to each of these forms. Thus we have:—

credentia	créance, *debt*	croyance, *belief*
hospitale	hôtel, *town-house, inn*	hôpital, *hospital*
potion-em	poison, *poison*	potion, *draught*
dotare	douer, *to give*	doter, to *endow*
L. L. soniare,	soin, besoin, *want, care*	besogne *business*
signum	seing, *signature*	signe, *sign*
natalis	natal, *natal*	Noël, *Christmas*
porticus	porche, *porch*	portique, *portico*
major	majeur, *of age*	maire, *mayor*
senior	sire, sieur	seigneur

§ 34. On the other hand, by the gradual impoverishment of the vocalism of the language, we find words from different etyma, having different meanings, but the same form:—

locare	louer, *to hire, let*
laudare	louer, *to praise*
falx	faux, *scythe*
falsus	faux, *false*
focus	feu, *fire*
fuit	feu, *late, deceased* *
novus	neuf, *new*
novem	neuf, *nine*
palatium	palais, *palace*
palatum	palais, *palate*
pagina	page, *page in a book*
παιδίον	page, *a boy*
tendere	tendre, *to span*
tenerum	tendre, *tender*
cingulum	sanglot, *girth*
singultus	sanglot, *sob*
causari	causer, *to cause*
G. kosen	causer, *to talk*
sonus	son, *sound*
suum	son, *his*

* This etymology explains why *feu* is never used in the plural.

carcer	chartre, f. *prison*
charta (ula)	chartre, f. *charter*
piscari	pêcher, *to fish*
peccare	pêcher, *to sin*
persica (arius)	pêcher, *peach-tree*
consuere	coudre, *to sow*
corylus	coudre, coudrier, *hazel*
maritus	mariage, *marriage*
mare	O. F. mariage, *service at sea*
coquus	queux, m. *cook*
cos	queux, m. *hone*
carpinus	charme, m. *witch-elm*
carmen	charme, m. *charm*
perca	perche, f. *perch* (*fish*)
pertica	perche, f. *perch* (*measure*)

§ 35. The etymology of these homonyms is of especial value in the case of nouns of different meanings and genders. They will be spoken of in the chapter on Nouns. Here only a few as specimens:—

somnus	le somme, *nap*
summa	la somme, *sum*
liber	le livre, *book*
libra	la livre, *pound*

This poverty of sounds has been the cause of the great facility of punning in French, giving thus an additional proof of the truth of Bacon's words: ' Men believe that their reason is lord over their words; but it happens, too, that words exercise a reciprocal and reactionary power over their intellect. Words, as a Tartar's bow, shoot back upon the understanding of the wisest, and mightily entangle and pervert the judgment.'

MORPHOLOGY.

ARTICLES.

§ 36. By a process common to all modern European languages, the demonstrative pronoun loses its purely demonstrative force, and is used for particularizing any common noun. In the Romance languages, the pronoun chosen for this purpose is the demonstrative *ille, illa*. Traces of the original force of this pronoun have been preserved in such phrases as: *Pour le coup, de la sorte, à l'instant même*. In the old language the article presents a great variety of forms, which at present have been reduced to *le* for the masculine and *la* for the feminine. The most usual Old French forms are:—

		Masc.	Fem.	M. and F. Picard.
Sing.	*Nom.*	li, l'	li, la, lai, l'	li, le
	Gen.	del, deu, dou, du, do	de la, de lai, de l'	de le, del
	Dat.	al, au, eu, ou	à la, à lai, ai lai, a l'	à le, al, el
	Acc.	lo, lou, lu, le, l'	la, lai, l'	le
Plur.	*Nom.*	li	les, li	li
	Gen.	dels, des	dels, des	des
	Dat.	als, as, aus	als, as	as
	Acc.	les	les	les

In Old French the article undergoes frequent contractions with prepositions and pronouns: *nel* (ne le), *nes* (ne les), *jel* (je les), *mes* (me les), *es* (en les), the latter of which is preserved in *bachelier ès lettres, ès mains*.

The modern language preserves only the contractions with *de* and *à*.

§ 37. The numeral *unus, una*, is used as indefinite article. Traces of this use are frequent in the conversational language of the Romans: *Unum vidi mortuum efferri* (Plaut. *Most.* iv. 3, 9). *Forte unam adspicio adolescentulam* (Terent. *And.* i. 1, 90). *Constitit ante oculos Naias una meos* (Ovid. *Her.* xv. 162).

Like the definite article, the indefinite has more closely preserved the Latin form in Old French:—

	Masc.	Fem.
Nom.	uns	une
Cas. Obliq.	un	une

Even a plural of this article is frequent in Old French : *unes grandes joes* (joues); *unes narines*; reminding of the Latin *una castra, unæ literæ.*

SUBSTANTIVES.

For convenience' sake we shall consider the derivation and gender of nouns together, and treat separately of declension.

§ 38. *Declension.*—The great variety of six cases for each number of the five Latin declensions appears even in the classical language somewhat reduced and simplified. For the dative and ablative are always identical in the plural, and frequently so in the singular; the nominative singular and accusative and vocative are frequently alike in form. The process of reducing the numerous cases and declensions shows itself in such nouns as *senatus, domus, plebs,* which seem to indicate a gradual merging of the fourth into the second, and of the fifth into the third declension.* The vulgar and mediæval Latin carry the process of simplification still farther, until in Modern French only two distinct forms remain, one for the singular, and a second for the plural, formed by the suffix *s* or *x*.

§ 39. The old French declension has preserved a much closer resemblance to the Latin declension. The feminines in *e* mute alone form all cases of the plural by adding *s* :—

corone, *corona*   voie, *via*
corone, *coronam*   voie, *viam*
corones, *coronæ*   voies, *viæ*
corones, *coronas*   voies, *vias*

All feminines not ending in *e* mute, and all masculines preserve a distinct form for the casus rectus (*cas sujet*) and for the casus obliqui (*cas régime*). The casus rectus of the sing. and the casus obl. of the plur. are formed by the suffix *s* :—

	Masc.			Fem.	
Sing. Nom.	murs	rois	chiens	flours	volontes
Cas. Obl.	mur	roi	chien	flour	volonte
Plur. Nom.	mur	roi	chien	flours	volentes
Cas. Obl.	murs	rois	chiens	flours	volentes

A number of nouns from *tor, toris,* and *o, onis,* have a still greater resemblance to the Latin inflection by shifting their accent :—

---

* The old ablatives *diu* (die) and *noctu* (nocte) indicate the same process.

Sing. Nom.	empereres, *imperător*	bers, *baro*
Cas. Obl.	empereór, *imperatōrem*	baron, *barōnem*
Plur. Nom.	empereor, *imperatōres*	baron, *barōnes*
Cas. Obl.	empereors, *imperatōres*	barons, *barōnes*

Thus are declined: *chanteres*, cantor, cas. obl. *chanteór*, cantorem; *sendre* or *sire*, senior, cas. obl. *seignor*, seniōrem; *salverres*, salvator, cas. obl. *salveór*; *traitres*, traitor. The Germanic *fels, fellon, Charles, Charlon,* and *gars, garçon,* of uncertain origin, and Greek *Estevenes* (Stephanus), *Estevenon; Pierres, Pierron,* follow this declension, the oblique cases of which became in course of time the ordinary nominatives: *garçon, felon, empereur, baron, seigneur.*

Some remnants are likewise found of the accusative singular in *am* of the first declension: nom. sing. *ante* (amita), acc. *antain*; *nonne* (nonna), *nonnain*.

§ 40. The origin of the suffix *s* for the nominative singular is explained by a mere reference to the nominative terminations of the Latin declensions. The suffix *s* appears in the nominative singular of all declensions (*Æneas, dominus, avis, pectus, flos, fructus, dies*). In Low Latin, nouns not ending in *s* gradually drop their peculiar suffix, and assume the one peculiar to the nominative. The origin of the *s* of the casus obliquus of the plural is still more apparent, for all Latin accusatives plural, with the exception of the neuters, end in *s*. The neuter being merged in the masculine, the only termination remaining was *s*.

The distinction between the casus rectus and casus obliquus was observed in French till the eleventh century. After that the suffix *s* (sometimes written *z*) was used for forming a different form for the plural.

The use of *x* as an inflectional letter was originally confined to words ending in *l*, and was appended after rejection of the *l* (vocalized in *u*): *fix=fils, max=maux, castiax=châteaux.*

§ 41. The Indo-Germanic suffix *s* for the nominative singular is without doubt a remnant of the pronominal root *sa* (Skt. and Goth. *să* (m.), *să* (f.); Greek ὁ, ἡ). In the nominative plural another inflectional *s* is added, which most likely has its origin in the same *sa*, so that the full original termination was *sasa*. Thus Skt. *vākh-s*, pl. *vak-as* (for *vak-sas*); Greek ὄπ-ς (ὄψ), pl. ὅπες; Lat. *voc-s* (vox), pl. *voc-es*.

§ 42. The genitive and dative are formed by placing the prepositions *de* and *à* (Lat. *de* and *ad*) before the casus obliquus. Even in classical Latin these prepositions were occasionally used with the noun in the ablative instead of the simple genitive or dative of the noun: *Si quis de nostris hominibus a genere isto abhorrens fuit* (Cic. *Flacc.* 41). *Themistocles noctu de servis suis quem habuit fidelissimum ad regem misit* (Nepos, *Them.* iv. 3). *De tuis innumerabilibus in me officiis erit hoc gratissumum* (Cic. *ad Fam.* xvi. 1, 2). *Habeatur sane orator, sed de minoribus* (Cic. *Opt. Gen. Or.* iv. 9). *Offerre se ad mortem* (Cic. *Tusc.* i. 15). *Scribas ad me quidquid veniet tibi in mentem* (Cic. *ad Att.* xi. 25). In Low Latin *de* and *ad* are used indiscriminately with any case. A reminiscence of the Latin case-endings is perhaps to be found in the frequent omission of the case-particles in Old French: *Le fils l'empereor de Constantinople qui frere sa fame est* (Ville-Hardouin). *Cist Josias fist ço que Deu plout* (2 Liv. des Rois). *Ne le dirai fame ne home* (Eustache d'Amiens). *Et la Roine l'esgarda, le Roi le mostra son Segnor* (Marie de France). In Modern French this omission of *de* and *à* has been preserved in *hotel-Dieu, fête-Dieu, Faubourg Saint-Antoine*; and in many names of places, as *Château-Thierry, Bar-le-Duc, Plessis-les-Tours*; also in *de par le roi* (de parte regis).

§ 43. *Derivation and Gender.*—French nouns are derived either direct from Latin nouns, or from infinitives, participles, adjectives, and prepositions, sometimes without, but more generally with, the aid of a suffix.

§ 44. French nouns derived from Latin nouns must be deduced from the Latin accusative as the case which invariably (with the exception of some neuters) shows the crude form. Although a few isolated forms (*corps*, corpus; *temps*, tempus; *on*, hom-o) seem to have preserved a Latin nominative, nevertheless the bulk of French nouns point to one of the oblique cases. *Comte* cannot be derived from *comes*, *nation* from *natio*, or *nuit* from *nox*; but they might as well be derived from a genitive, dative, or ablative. But it is most unlikely that the form which was to serve for all cases should be derived from a case of comparatively rare use, instead of the one most frequent in use. Our feeling for language rejects the genitive, dative, and ablative, and such decided accusative forms as *homme* (hominem), *pomme* (pomum), *femme* (feminam), *mon* (meum), *ton* (tuum), *son* (suum), *rien* (rem), confirm the view that the Latin accusative is the normal case which has supplied the form of French words. When giving the Latin etymon of a French noun, the accusative should therefore be given, unless some other case appears to have supplied the French form.

§ 45. The gender of substantives is determined either by the meaning or by the suffix.

§ 46. *Gender determined by meaning.*—(*a*) The names of

males, months, and winds are masculine both in Latin and French.

Exceptions.—The names of some males, chiefly such as have changed an abstract meaning into a concrete, are feminines: *une aide, la dupe, la sentinelle, la recrue, la cornette, la taille, la haute-contre, la clarinette* (clarionet, clarionet-player). Compare Lat. *operæ*, works, workmen. The names of festivals are feminines, *la fête de* having to be supplied to *la Toussaint, la Saint-Jean, la Saint-Michel. La bise, la tramontane, la mousson, la brise.*

(*b.*) The names of trees and shrubs are masculine in French, but feminine in Latin. This change of gender is probably attributable to the custom of the spoken Roman language. *Cupressus, laurus,* and *platanus* are used as masculine in archaic Latin. On the other hand, the following are feminine in French: *l'yeuse, l'ébène, la bourdaine, l'hièble, la viorne, l'épine, la ronce, la vigne.*

(*c.*) The names of female persons and animals are feminine in both languages.

(*d.*) By far the largest number of abstracta are feminine in both languages. Exceptions are frequent: *le vice*, vitium; *l'égoïsme*; *le courage*, L. L. coragium (cor); all in *isme* and *asme*, etc.

§ 47. *Gender determined by Suffixes.*—As the gender was in Latin determined by the suffix, which in French nouns derived from Latin nouns is either dropped entirely, or so weakened as to lose the force of a suffix, it follows that the modern substantives become, so to speak, genderless. So powerful, nevertheless, was the genius of the Roman language, that the French genders mainly coincide with the Latin genders. Masculines and feminines have retained their original genders; all communia and most neuters have become masculines. The etymology of French nouns is, therefore, a far safer guide in ascertaining the gender of substantives than their terminations. The termination *-age*, for instance, is enumerated in all French grammars as a masculine termination. But it is so only when it can be traced back to the Latin *-aticum* (*-agium*): *le voyage* (viaticum), *le courage* (coragium). On the other hand, *rage* (rabies), *image* (imago), *cage* (cavea), *plage* (plaga), *ambages* (ambages), *hypallage* (ὑπαλλαγή) are feminine, following the gender of their respective etyma. In the same manner those in *-oire* are masculine when derived from *-orium*: *oratoire, prétoire, purgatoire*; and feminine when derived from *-oria*: *écritoire, nageoire, mâchoire*. Those in *-ule* are masculine when derived from -*ulus*, -*ulum*: *corpuscule, crépuscule, monticule*; and feminine when derived from -*ula*: *canicule, capsule, formule*.

§ 48. The principal deviations from the Latin gender are :—

A. *Change of Masculines into Feminines.*

(*a.*) Masculines of the first Latin declension rarely change their gender : *la Marne* (Matrona, *m.*), *la planète* (planetæ, *pl. m.*), *la comète* (cometes, *m.*).

(*b.*) Some masculines of the second and fourth declensions become feminines: *la mousse* (muscus, *m.*), *la rame* (ramus, *m.*), *la merluche* (maris lucius, *m.*), *l'auge* (alveus, *m.*), *la grenouille* (ranunculus, *m.*), *la graille* (graculus, *m.*), *l'hièble* (ebulus, *m.*), *l'asperge* (asparagus, *m.*), *l'émeraude* (smaragdus, *m.*), *l'opale* (opalus, *m.*), *l'obole* (obolus, *m.*), *l'arche* (arcus, *m.*), *la figue* (ficus, *m.* as fruit, *f.* as tree). The final mute *e* characterises this change of gender.

(*c.*) Masculines of the third declension which become feminine are generally marked by the final mute *e*: *la Loire* (Liger, ĕris, *m.*), *la chartre* (carcer, ĕris, *m.*), *la pouce* (pumex, ĭcis, *m.*), *la puce* (pulex, ĭcis, *m.*), *la herse* (irpex, ĭcis, *m.*), *l'écorce* (cortex, ĭcis, *m.*), *la moustache* (μύσταξ, ακος, *m.*), *la tourtre* (turtur, ŭris, *m.*), *la poudre* (pulvis, ĕris, *m.*), *la cendre* (cinis, ĕris). Of these, *pulvis, cinis, cortex,* and *pumex,* occur, however, occasionally as feminines, especially in poets.

(*d.*) The abstracta in *or*, *ōris*, have, without exception, exchanged their masculine Latin gender for a French feminine: *Couleur, douleur, faveur, fureur,* without taking the mute *e*, which generally characterises these words.

(*e.*) A few other nouns follow this example, and exchange their masculine for a feminine gender, without taking a final *e* mute: *la dent* (dens, *m.*), *la souris* (sorex, ĭcis, *m.*), *la brebis* (vervex, ēcis, *m.*), *la fleur* (flos, ōris, *m.*), *les mœurs* (mores, *m.*), *la paroi* (paries, *m.*), *les annales*, f. (annales, *m.*).

B. *Change of Feminines into Masculines.*

(*a.*) Feminines of the first declension which become masculines by throwing off their original termination: *l'épi* (spica), *le lézard* (lacerta, *f.*), *le fétu* (festuca, *f.*), *le tilleul* (tiliola, *f.*), *le Languedoc* (from lingua, *f.*), *le daim* (dama, *f.*, used by Virgil as *m.*).

A few retain their original termination: *le lierre* (hedera, *f.*), *l'ongle* (ungula, *f.*), *le rossignol* (lusciniola, *f.*), *le piége* (pedica, *f.*), *l'orchestre* (orchestra, *f.*), *le dimanche* (dominica, sc. dies), *les thermes* (thermæ, *f.*), *le litre* (ἡ λίτρα).

With these must not be confounded the large class of substantives derived immediately from the crude form of the verb without the addition of any suffix, as *le plant, le repos* (from *plant-er, repos-er*), and which must not be deduced from Latin substantives. Others again point to unusual or low Latin forms as their etyma. Thus *le délice* is from *delicium*, not from *deliciæ*; *le moulin* not from *molina*, but from *molinum*; *l'antidote* not from *antidotus* (f.), but from *antidotum*.

(*b.*) Some feminines of the second and fourth declensions, chiefly the names of trees, become masculines: *le cyprès* (cupressus), *le buis* (buxus, *f.* and buxum, *n.*), *le pin* (pinus, *f.*), *le myrte* (myrtus, *f.*), *l'aune* (alnus, *f.*), *le plane, le platane* (platanus, *f.*), *le portique, le porche* (porticus, *f.*), *le dôme* (domus, *f.*), and the compounds of ὁδός: *le synode* (synodus, *f.*), *l'exode* (exodus, *f.*), with some others from the Greek: *le dialecte* (dialectus, *f.*), *le diamètre* (diametrus, *f.*), *l'atome* (atomus, *f.*), *le perimètre* (perimetrus, *f.*), *le paragraphe* (paragraphus, *f.*), *l'abîme* (abyssus, *f.*, abyssimus?).

Le période, a space of time; *la période*, period in grammar, phrase.

(*c.*) A few feminines of the third declension become masculines: *l'arbre* (arbor, ŏris, *f.*), *le sort* (sors, sortis, *f.*), *l'art* (ars, artis, *f.*), *le salut* (salus, ūtis, *f.*), *le palus* (palus, ūdis, *f.*), *l'appendice* (appendix, ĭcis, *f.*), *le sphynx* (sphynx, gis, *f.*), *le soupçon* (suspicio, onis, *f.*), *le poison* (potio, ōnis, *f.*), *le vertige* (vertigo, ĭnis, *f.*), *le cartilage* (cartilago, inis, *f.*), *le diocèse* (diœcesis, *f.*), *le jaspe* (iaspis, ĭdis, *f.*), *le rets* (retis, *f.*), *l'iris* (iris, *f.*).

Le cinabre is from *cinnabari*, m., and not from *cinnabaris*, f., *le chanvre* from *cannabus*, m., and not from *cannabis*, f.

(*d.*) Substantives of common gender, as has been observed before, take in French generally the masculine gender: *chien* (canis), *le serpent* (serpen-tem); but *la grue* (grus, *c.*) and *la perdrix* (perdrix, *c.*) become feminines.

§ 49. C. *French Gender of Latin Neuters.*

(*a.*) No principle has as yet been discovered, by which we might be guided in distinguishing neuters which become feminine from those that become masculine. A large number of the feminines are derived from Latin plurals: *merveille* (mirabilia), *entrailles* (intra, and thence, perhaps, *intralia*), *épousailles* (sponsalia), *aumaille* (animalia), *arme* (arma, orum), *muraille* (muralia), *volaille* (volatilia). The majority of them have the distinguishing mark of the final *e* mute : *huile* (oleum), *lèvre* (labrum), *horloge* (horologium), *étable* (stabulum), *joie* (gaudium), *étude* (studium), *tourmente* (tormentum), *ache* (apium), *viorne* (viburnum), *pomme* (pomum), *poire* (pirum), *prune* (prunum), *mûre* (morum), *cymbale* (cymbalum), *toise* (tensum), *pointe* (punctum), *réponse* (responsum), *épithète* (epitheton), *voile* (velum), *feuille* (folium), *dépouille* (spolium), together with a number of words ending in *aie* (*etum*) : *saussaie* (salicetum), *boulaie* (betuletum), *roseraie* (rosaretum).

Neuters of the third declension which are in French feminine : *étamine* (stamen), *pécore* (pecus, ora), *pair* (par, paria), and the neuter plurals mentioned before : *merveille, volaille, muraille,* etc.

(*b.*) By far the largest number of Latin neuters, amongst them the names of metals and fruits, assume in French the masculine gender : *or* (aurum), *plomb* (plumbum), *argent* (argentum), *métal* (metallum), *vin* (vinum), *ail* (allium), *huis* (ostium), *bras* (bracchium), *prix* (pretium), *pré* (pratum), *ciel* (cœlum), *vœu* (votum), *œuf* (ovum), *fait* (factum), *décret* (decretum), *manuscrit* (manuscriptum), *écu* (scutum), *arbuste* (arbustum), *prodige* (prodigium), *règne* (regnum), *signe* (signum), *siècle* (sæculum), *vice* (vitium). Words of the third declension : *autel* (altare), *airain* (æramen), *nom* (nomen), *temps* (tempus), *cœur* (cor), *cadavre* (cadaver), *marbre* (marmor), *volume* (volumen), *vase* (vas, vasa, orum), *diplôme* (diploma), *charme* (carmen).

§ 50.   D. *Double Forms and French Communia.*

(*a.*) From a few Latin nouns are derived a French masculine and feminine :—

vitrum, *n.*	le verre	la vitre
granum, *n.*	le grain	la graine
limax, *g. c.*	le limas	la limace
dama, *f.*	le dain	la daine

(*b.*) The number of substantives of common gender, especially of those denoting persons, is considerable : *aristocrate, élève, artiste, camarade, émule, esclave, interprète, patriote, compatriote, pupille, adversaire, locataire, pensionnaire, propriétaire, dépositaire, enfant, enthousiaste, démoniaque, sauvage, volage, rebelle, Belge, Russe, Scythe, Spartiate, Vandale,* etc.

§ 51. (*c.*) A distinction has been made by grammarians in the use of the masculine and feminine of some substantives of common gender, which generally is based on some change in

GENDER, DERIVATION.

the meaning. Sometimes the one gender is assigned to the whole, whilst the other is reserved for the part (*pars pro toto*), or the agent is expressed by the masculine, and the instrument by the feminine. Custom, or, still more frequently, the whims of grammarians, have made distinctions which are not recognised by scientific philologists and lexicographers:—

aquila	un aigle, *bird of prey*	une aigle, *standard*
viper	le givre, *snake, in heraldry*	la givre, *hoar-frost*
velum	le voile, *veil*	la voile, *sail*
pendulum	le pendule, *pendulum*	la pendule, *clock*
picus (*woodpecker*)	le pique, *spade, in cards*	la pique, *pike, weapon*
vapor	le vapeur, *steamer*	la vapeur, *steam*
copula	un couple, *man and wife*	une couple, *a pair*
fourbjan (O. H. G.)	le fourbe, *deceiver*	la fourbe, *deception*
wart-en (G.)	le garde, *keeper*	la garde, *guard*
pestis	le peste, *troublesome boy*	la peste, *pestilence*
modus	le mode, *mode, manner of being*	la mode, *fashion*
insign-is	un enseigne, *subaltern officer*	une enseigne, *standard*
(tuba ?)	un trompette, *a trumpeter*	une trompette, *trumpet*
adjut-us	un aide, *assistant*	une aide, *help*
manus opera (O. H. G. vitan ?)	le manœuvre, *workman* le guide, *guide*	la manœuvre, *manœuvre* les guides, f. *reins*
merced-em	le merci, *thanks*	la merci, *mercy*
cornu, corneta	le cornette, *cornet (officer)*	la cornette, *standard*
memoria	le mémoire, *memorandum, bill*	la mémoire, *memory*
ἠχώ	un echo, *echo*	Echo, f. *name of a nymph*
officium	un office, *office, appointment*	une office, *pantry*

§ 52. (*d*.) With these must not be confounded substantives derived from the same etymon, but from different genders:—

le critique, *criticus*	la critique, *critica* (sc. *ars*)
le poste, *positum*	la poste, *posita* (sc. *statio*)
le prétexte, *prætextum*	la prétexte, *prætexta* (sc. *toga*)
le parallèle, *parallelon*	la parallèle, *parallela* (sc. *linea*)
le manche, *mancum*	la manche, *manca*
le délice, *delicium*	les délices, f. *deliciæ*
le baignoir, *balneatorium*	la baignoire, *balneatoria*
le satire, *satyrus*	la satire, *satira*

§ 53. (*e*.) The following homonyms are derived from different etyma, which account for their different genders and meaning:—

Masc.	Fem.
un aune (alnus), *alder-tree*	une aune (ulna), *ell*
le barbe (Barbaria), *Barbary horse*	la barbe (barba), *beard*
le carpe (carpus), *root of the hand*	la carpe (O. H. G. charpho, Lat. carpio), *a carp*
le foudre (G. fuder), *tun*	la foudre (fulgur), *thunderbolt*
le greffe (graphium), *record-office*	la greffe (E. to graft), *shoot*
le livre (liber), *book*	la livre (libra), *pound*

le capre (capere), *pirate*
le moule (modulus), *mould*
le mousse (mustus, Sp. mozo), *cabin boy*
le page (παιδίον), *boy*
le palme (palmus), *span*

le somme (somnus), *sleep*
le souris (subridere), *smile*
le tour (tornus), *turn*
le vase (vas), *vase*
le vague, *adj.* (vagus), *vague*
l'heur (augurium), *luck**

la câpre (capparis), *caper*
la moule (O. H. G. muscula), *mussel*
la mousse (G. moos), *moss*
la page (pagina), *page in a book*
la palme (palma), *branch of palm-tree*

la somme (summa), *sum*
la souris (sorex), *mouse*
la tour (turris), *tower*
la vase (O. H. G. waso), *mud*
la vague (G. woge), *wave*
l'heure (hora), *hour*

§ 54. *Derivation of Substantives.*—The majority of French substantives are derived from Latin substantives, adjectives, and verbs. Only one is derived from a pronoun: *l'identité* (idem); and only three from prepositions: *la contrée* (contra), *les entrailles* (intra), *l'avantage* (avant = ab ante). More frequently substantives are derived from Latin adjectives: *soir* (serus), *aube* (alba), *droit* (directum), *hôpital, hôtel* (hospitalis), *cardinal* (cardinalis).

§ 55. *Derivation of Substantives direct from Latin Verbs.*—Greater variety is shown in the process of deriving French substantives from Latin verbs. Here we find forms derived from the participle present, from the participle perfect, the infinitive and the crude form of the verb, without the addition of any suffix.

(*a.*) From the present participle are derived chiefly the names of male persons in *ent* and *ant*, which occasionally is

---

* From *heur*, luck, are derived *bonheur* (bonum augurium), *malheur* (malum augurium), *heureux* (augurosus). The derivation from *bona hora, mala hora,* is contradicted by the gender, the termination, and the meaning. The forms of the cognate languages likewise disprove it. The initial *h* is of later origin, probably prefixed from a mistaken notion as to their etymology. The langue d'Oïl wrote *eur* and *eureus*. *Augurosus* is found in Low-Latin, but not *horosus*. Of still greater importance is the *ora-culum*, for *augura-culum*, which reminds of the English *Austin* for *August-in*. In the time of Corneille *heure* (hour) and *heur* (luck) were still two words with very distinct meaning and spelling. See, for instance, the following passages:—

Qui l'eût dit ?—que notre *heur* fut si proche
Et sitôt se perdît.
Le Cid iii. 4.

Tu t'en souviens, Cinna ; tant d'*heur* et tant de gloire
Ne peuvent pas sitôt sortir de ta mémoire.
Cinna v. 1.

Puisse le juste ciel, content de ma ruine,
Combler d'*heur* et de jours Polyeucte et Pauline.
Polyeucte ii. 2.

And the following, quoted by Littré from Bercheure :—

Hercules, estendue sa main, dist que il acceptoit bien celi *aür*.

spelled *and*: *sergent* (servientem), *régent*, *président*, *résident*, *amant*, *manant* (manentem),* *marchand* (mercantem), *adolescent*; and the following two feminines: *servante* (servientem), *gouvernante* (gubernantem).

Also names of things and abstract nouns of the masculine gender are derived from the present participle: *orient*, *occident*, *torrent*, *levant*, *couchant*, *courant*, *tranchant*, *vivant* (du vivant de), *séant* (sur mon séant), *montant*, *semblant* (faire semblant), *ascendant*, *penchant*, *pendant*, *accident*, *incident*.

The few feminines are properly adjectives in the feminine form, which are easily explained by the ellipsis of a substantive; as, *la patente* (lettre), *la constituante* (assemblée), *la sécante* (ligne).

The suffix *-ant* (when appended to crude forms ending in a vowel, *-nt*) is found in all Indo-Germanic languages, and is used for the formation of active participles, including the participles of the Greek future and aorist: λύο-ντ-, λύσα-ντ-, λύσο-ντ-, δείκνυ-ντ-, φύγο-ντ-. The formation of substantives and adjectives by means of this suffix takes place also in Greek: ὀ-δό-ντ-, ἄκ-οντ-, γέρ-οντ-, ἐκ-όντ-; and still more frequently in Latin: *silent-ium*, *sapient-ia*, *licent-ia*, *abundant-ia*, *prudent-ia*, *Constant-ius*, *Fulgent-ius*, *Florent-ia*, *volunt-arius*, *frequent-*, *recent-*, *petulant-*, *po-cul-ent-u-s*, *vinol-ent-u-s*, *vi-ol-ent-u-s*, *pest-il-ent-u-s*, *esc-ul-ent-u-s*, *fraud-ul-ent-u-s*, *luc-ul-ent-u-s*, *cru-ent-u-s*.

§ 56. (*b*.) A very large number of substantives of the feminine gender are derived from the past participle: *allée*, *arrivée*, *avancée*, *bordée*, *chevauchée*, *couvée*, *croisée*, *dictée*, *durée*, *entrée*, *fumée*, *gelée*, *levée*, *montée*, *nichée*, *pensée*, *renommée*, *tournée*, *tranchée*, *rangée*, *veillée*, *partie*, *saisie*, *sallie*, *sortie*, *issue*, *venue*, *avenue*, *tenue*, *retenue*, *fuite* (from the O. F. p. p. *fuit*), *découverte*, *contrainte*, *feinte*, *prise*, *surprise*, *mise*, *remise*, *défaite*, *conduite*. A few prefer the form of the Latin participle: *promesse* (promissa), *requête*, *enquête*, *quête* (quæsita), *perte* (perdita), *dette* (debita), *rente* (reddita). Analogous to these are formed: *fente* (fendere), *pente* (pendere), *tente* (tendere), *attente* (attendere), *descente* (descendere), *ponte* (ponere), *fonte* (fundere).

A few, derived from the neuter form of the Latin past participle, are of the masculine gender. They end all in *t*: *avocat*, *adjoint*, *décret*, *objet*, *crédit*, *dépôt*, *impôt*, *réduit*, *écrit*,

---

* So that *manant* originally means a man who remains in a place, a serf, villain.

couvert. But *clos* (clausum), *aperçu, arrêté, négligé, crû, tissu, revenu*, are masculine substantives in the form of French past participles.

§ 57. (*c.*) The infinitive supplies a large number of substantives of the masculine gender: *baiser, plaisir, souvenir, pouvoir, vivre*(*s*), *loisir, devoir, savoir, loyer, manger, boire, souper, sourire, avenir, repentir, être*.

§ 58. (*d.*) The crude form of the verb is used as a substantive of the masculine gender:—

Substantive.	Verb.	Etymon.
l'aboi	aboyer	(ad-)baubari
l'accord	accorder	accordare
l'accueil	accueillir	colligere
l'appel	appeler	appellare
le cri	crier	quiritare
le convoi	convoyer (O. F.)	conviare
le décor	décorer	decorare
le déclin	décliner	declinare
le dédain	dédaigner	dedignari
le dégât	dégâter	devastare
le dégel	dégeler	gelare
le débat	débattre	debatuere
le dégout	dégoûter	degustare
le départ	départir	partiri
le désir	désirer	desiderare
le destin	destiner	destinare
le détail	détailler	taleare
le deuil	douloir	dolere
l'envoi	envoyer	inviare
l'éclair	éclairer	exclarare
l'emploi	employer	implicare
l'éveil	éveiller	evigilare
le maintien	maintenir	manu-tenere
l'octroi	octroyer	auctorare
le pardon	pardonner	perdonare
le parfum	parfumer	fumare
le port*	porter	portare
le présent	présenter	præsentare
le protêt	protester	protestari
le ragoût	ragoûter	regustare
le rapport	rapporter	apportare
le recel	recéler	celare
le réchaud	réchauffer	calefacere
le récit	réciter	recitare
le refus	refuser	refutare
le regret	regretter	requiritare
le renom	renommer	nominare
le renvoi	renvoyer	inviare

* Postage, carriage; not to be confounded with *le port* (portus).

GENDER, DERIVATION.

Substantive.	Verb.	Etymon.
le report	reporter	reportare
le repos	reposer	pausare
le retard	retarder	retardare
le réveil	réveiller	vigilare
le secours	secourir	succurrere
le souci	soucier	sollicitare
le surcroît	croître	crescere
le viol	violer	violare
le vol	vouloir	velle (like *volere*)
le vol	voler	volare

This process of forming substantives from verbs was obviously the easiest and readiest method which offered itself to the Latin-speaking nations during the time of the morphological decay of the Roman language. The numerous examples above show that the length of a word is a treacherous guide as to its etymology. The derivative is certainly in most cases longer than the root or stem, and the presence of a suffix a proof that the word is derived from one which has no such suffix. But in this instance the process is reversed, and the crude form of the verb used as a substantive must be considered as derived from the verb by throwing off the suffix of the infinitive.

§ 59. (*e*.) The suffix *e* (Latin *a*) is frequently added to the crude form of a verb and has the force of giving to it a substantive meaning, expressing an act. (Compare *fug-ere, fug-a*.) These substantives are of the feminine gender, excepting those given in the next paragraph :—

French Substantive.	French Verb.	Etymon.
l'adresse	adresser	directus
l'affiche	afficher	fixare
l'aide	aider	adjutare
l'amende	amender	emendare
l'annonce	annoncer	annuntiare
l'approche	approcher	appropiare
l'avance	avancer	ab-ante
la baisse	baisser	bassus
la charge	charger	carricare
la consigne	consigner	consignare
la conteste	contester	contestari
la couche	coucher	collocare
la débauche	débaucher	debacchari ?
la décharge	décharger	carricare
la dépêche	dépêcher	pedica, depedicare ?
la dépense	dépenser	dispensare
la dépouille	dépouiller	spoliare
la détrempe	détremper	temperare
la dispute	disputer	disputare
les entraves	entraver	trabs, trabis (intrabare?)
l'épouvante	épouvanter	pavere (expaventare)

French Substantive.	French Verb.	Etymon.
l'épreuve	éprouver	probare
l'estime	estimer	æstimare
l'excuse	excuser	excusare
la fatigue	fatiguer	fatigare
la faute	fauter (O. F.)	fallere (fallitare?)
l'intrigue	intriguer	intricare
la loge	loger	locare
la nage	nager	navigare
l'offre	offrir	offere (*for* offerrere)
la pêche	pêcher	piscari
la presse	presser	pressare
la recherche	rechercher	circare
la rencontre	rencontrer	in-contra
la réclame	réclamer	reclamare
la réserve	réserver	reservare
la touche	toucher	taxare (*augmentat. from* tango, tactum)
la tourmente*	tourmenter	tormentum
la trempe	tremper	temperare

(*f.*) To this general law a few nouns are exceptions, which remind of the Latin *scrib-a* from *scrib-ĕre*, *incol-a* from *incol-ĕre*, inasmuch as they seem either to have been originally abstract nouns, or nouns of common gender:—

l'élève	élever	elevare
le juge	juger	judicare
le fourbe	fourbir	O.H.G. furbjan

§ 60. But no analogy can be found for the following, which take the feminine suffix *e*, and nevertheless retain the neuter gender of the crude-form substantives:—

le blâme	blamer	blasphemare
le change	changer	cambiare
le compte	compter	computare
le conte	conter	
le décompte	décompter	
un escompte	escompter	
le doute	douter	dubitare
le risque	risquer	resecare
le reproche	reprocher	repropiare (?)
le reste	rester	restare
le rêve	rêver	rabere, rabies
le réverbère	réverbérer	reverberare
le souffle	souffler	sufflare
le trouble	troubler	turbulare

* The termination and gender are a proof that *la tourmente* is derived from the French verb, and not from the Latin noun. From *tormentum* is derived *le tourment*.

GENDER, DERIVATION.

§ 61. *Derivation of Substantives from Verbs by means of Suffixes.*—In general it may be said of the Romance languages that they are poor in roots but rich in derivatives. Although a great many Latin suffixes in course of time have become so torpid as to be either entirely incapable of producing new derivatives or in very small numbers, other suffixes have shown a productiveness far surpassing anything in the Latin or the Germanic languages. The Germanic languages justly boast of their great facility for forming compound words, which, however, is frequently the cause of tumidity and awkwardness in style. The great treasures of derivatives of the Romance languages more than compensate for their inferior powers of composition. More than one suffix is frequently added to the same word, thus modifying the radical in the most various and delicate ways. Thus the name *Roma* supplies the following derivatives: *Rome, romain (-aine), romainement, roman, romance, romancier, romanesque, romanesquement, romantique, romantisme, romantiquement,* besides many others not in ordinary use. From the one word *caballus* are derived *cheval, chevalier, chevalière, chevaleresque, chevaleresquement, chevaler, chevalet, chevalerie, chevalement, chevaline, chevauchage, chevauchant, chevauchée, chevauchement, chevaucher, chevauchons, cavalcade, cavalcadour, cavale, cavalerie, cavalier, cavalière, cavalièrement.* The English language stands in this respect midway between the other Germanic and the Romance languages. From the German it has preserved a greater facility of forming compounds than the Romance languages, but far inferior to that of the other Germanic tongues. On the other hand, it makes up for its great poverty of suffixes by introducing the Romance derivatives ready-made.

Suffixes which retain their formative power in French are appended to the crude form of the verb; as, *alli-er, alli-ance*. Frequently, for the sake of euphony, *e* is used as a connecting vowel; as, *entend-re, entend-e-ment*. In verbs of the second conjugation which have the inflection of inchoatives, the suffix is appended to the inchoative form with the intervention of the connecting vowel *e*: *arrond-ir, arrond-iss-e-ment*. Some suffixes, on the other hand, are appended to the participle present; as, *pes-er*, part. pres. *pes-ant*, subst. *pes-ant-eur*.

§ 62. Lat. **tor, sor,** *masc.*; **trix, issa, osa,** *fem.*
Fr. **teur, seur, tre, eur,** *masc.*; **trice, esse, euse,** *fem.*

The Latin suffix *tor* was used for forming nomina agentis of the masculine gender from verbal roots: *ama-tor, crea-tor,*

D

audi-tor. This suffix was changed frequently into *sor*; *cens-or* for *cens-tor* (from *censeo*, root *cens-*), *spon-sor* for *spond-tor* (from *spondeo*, root *spond*). Many Latin substantives formed with this suffix pass into French, preserving both their gender and meaning: *amateur, créateur, débiteur, auditeur, serviteur, imitateur, acteur, fauteur, protecteur, précurseur, censeur*. In a few instances the long vowel of the termination is shortened; as, *chantre* (cantor), *peintre* (pictor), *traître* (traditor), *pâtre* (pastor), *ancêtres* (antecessores), a process which this suffix has undergone as well in Latin in *pa-ter*, *ma-ter*, *fra-ter*. In substantives formed from verbs of the *a* and *i* conjugations, the *t* is frequently thrown out: *gouverneur* (gubernator), *jongleur* (joculator), *pécheur* (peccator), *sauveur* (salvator), *vendeur* (venditor), *dormeur* (dormitor).

This suffix retains its formative power in this latter form, and is appended to the crude form as it appears in the participle present: *danseur, colporteur, coureur, défendeur, couvreur, acquéreur, entrepreneur, faiseur, diseur, liseur, confiseur, connaisseur, rieur, buveur*. From verbs of the inchoative form: *blanchisseur, polisseur, ravisseur, fournisseur, abrutisseur, fourbisseur, nourrisseur*.

The Latin nouns in *tor* form a feminine in *trix*, to which the French form in *ice* corresponds: *inventrice, accusatrice, bienfaitrice, directrice, impératrice*. Most names of female persons take in Low Latin the suffix *issa* (French *esse*): *abbat-issa, sacerdot-issa, diacon-issa, œthiop-issa, arab-issa, prophet-issa*, are found in the Fathers. This suffix strongly reminds of the formation of some Greek feminines: βασιλ-εύς, βασίλ-ισσα; χαρί-εις, χαρί-εσσα. Although this Greek formation may have had some influence on the corresponding forms in patristic Latin, still there is no reason to suppose why it should have been taken from the Greek. Many Etruscan names of women end in *-isa, -asa*, and *-esa*: *Athial-isa, Eilial-isa, Atainal-isa, Lar-isa, Latin-isa, Latinial-isa, Marcan-isa, Apic-esa, Capin-esa, Sepi-esa, At-esa, Herm-esa, Laucan-esa, Achuni-asa, Lent-asa*. In French we have: *prêtresse, traîtresse, pécheresse, vengeresse*, and, without any respect to the suffix of the masculine, *abbesse, princesse, comtesse, tigresse, ânesse, prophétesse, négresse, maîtresse, druidesse, chanoinesse, hôtesse, pairesse, duchesse, déesse*. Those nouns which append the suffix to the crude form of the verb as it shows itself in the participle present, make their feminine in *euse* (Lat. *osa*): *buv-eur, buv-euse* (*buv-ant*), *caus-eur, euse* (*caus-ant*), *dans-eur, euse* (*dans-ant*), *glan-eur, euse* (*glan-ant*), *port-*

eur, euse (port-ant), ment-eur, euse (ment-ant), quêt-eur, euse (quêt-ant).

§ 63. Lat. **men, mentum,** *neut.*
Fr. **aim, ain, ime, ume, ment,** *masc.*

The Latin suffix *men* (enlarged *mentum*), added to verbs, expresses the instrument by which the action of the verb is carried into effect. In the old language the simple suffix *men* was more usual, but its power being gradually weakened, it was reinforced by the secondary suffix *tum*. This is a process of frequent occurrence in all languages. Thus, in English, the primary suffix *ic* begins to be more and more usually reinforced by the secondary suffix *al* : *idiomat-ic-al, problemat-ic-al, class-ic-al, diabol-ic-al.* The Latin nouns *ag-men, ful-men, gra-men, o-men, sta-men,* are all good old words in which the primary suffix has remained in its original state. But even in the classical period we find side by side *frag-men* and *frag-mentum, muni-men* and *muni-mentum, cognomen* and *cogno-mentum, vela-men* and *vela-mentum.* The enlarged suffix gradually displaces the simple suffix, and at a later period we find nouns formed in *mentum* which have not passed through the preliminary formation in *men* : *concre-mentum, excre-mentum, decre-mentum, imple-mentum;* till at last we find formations like *regi-mentum, jura-mentum, cogita-mentum.*

From this it will be apparent that the primary suffix *men* could not retain its formative power in the modern languages. A very small number of nouns in *-men* pass into French with a more or less mutilated suffix: *airain* (æramen), *essaim* (examen), *nourrain* (nutrimen), *lien* (ligamen), *crime* (crimen), *volume* (volumen), *bitume* (bitumen), *charme* (carmen), *germe* (germen), *nom* (nomen).

The enlarged form *mentum,* on the other hand, has become one of the most prolific suffixes of the French language for the formation of masculine substantives from verbs.

Direct from the Latin are: *ligament, ornement, aliment, détriment, argument, document, monument, fragment, segment, ferment, tourment, moment, froment.*

Words of modern formation append *ment* to the verbal stem, generally with the intervention of the connecting vowel *e* : *bêl-e-ment, hurl-e-ment, dévou-e-ment, accabl-e-ment, acharn-e-ment, commenc-e-ment, habill-e-ment, épuis-e-ment, soulèv-e-ment, bégai-e-ment, deblai-e-ment, aboi-e-ment, mani-e-ment, entend-e-ment, abatt-e-ment, content-e-ment, vêt-e-ment, roul-e-ment, gazouill-e-ment;* and of inchoative forms, *abrut-iss-e-*

ment, accompl-iss-e-ment, rug-iss-e-ment, arrond-iss-e-ment. But the following are exceptions: *blanch-i-ment, bât-i-ment, garn-i-ment, assort-i-ment.* Derivatives from verbs in *ir* which have not the inchoative form, take sometimes *i-ment* sometimes *e-ment*: *consent-e-ment, recueill-e-ment, tressaill-e-ment, sent-i-ment, assent-i-ment, pressent-i-ment, ressent-i-ment, compart-i-ment.* From *connaître* is formed *connaissement*, and from *croître, accroissement, décroissement*; from *bruire, bruissement.* *Ameublement* is from the simple verb *meubler*, not to be confounded with *ameublissement* (mellowing of lands) from *ameublir* (agricult. term). In *châti(e)ment* the short connecting vowel *e* is absorbed by the long *i*.

§ 64. Lat. **or** (gen. **ōris**), *masc.*
Fr. **eur** (O. F. **our**), *masc. and fem.*

The majority of substantives in *eur* are taken direct from Latin nouns in *or*, and express a state or quality of being or acting. They are mostly abstracta, and of the feminine gender:* *ardeur, chaleur, clameur, couleur, ferveur, fureur, langueur, pudeur, rigueur, splendeur, sueur* (sudor), *torpeur.* The Old French termination *our* has been preserved in *amour* and *labour*. The number of Latin words has been greatly increased by a large number of abstract nouns formed from adjectives and participles present: *aigreur, ampleur, blancheur, fadeur, grandeur, grosseur, laideur, largeur, longueur, lenteur, profondeur, rondeur, douceur, pesanteur* (*pesant*), *épaisseur, froideur, tiédeur, puanteur* (*puant*).

The different manner in which the descriptive grammarian and the comparative grammarian class the various suffixes, is well illustrated by this one. The descriptive grammarian mechanically classes under this head nouns like *sauveur* (salvator), *pêcheur* (peccator), which the comparative grammarian ranges with nouns in *teur*. Similarly *heur* (augurium) and its compounds, *bonheur, malheur, déshonneur*, are classed with nouns in *eur*. Now, although they terminate in *eur*, this *eur* is no suffix, but, on the contrary, the root of the word, deprived of its Latin suffix *ium*. As the suffix has the power of determining the gender, it follows that these words must be French masculines, being original Latin neuters without a formative French suffix.

The concrete nouns in *eur* are masculines. The only abstract noun in *or* which retains its Latin gender is *l'honneur*.

---

* This remarkable change of gender has been discussed before, § 48.

§ 65. Lat. **icius,** *masc.*; **icium,** *neut.*
Fr. **is,** *masc.*

The suffix *icius, icium* (Fr. *is*) is used in Latin for forming adjectives from substantives meaning 'belonging to': *tribunicius, ficticius, pellicius, adventicius*. In French it is generally added to verbal stems, whilst the feminine form *icia* (*isse*) prefers nominal stems. All derivatives in *is* are of the masculine gender: *l'abatis* (abattre), *l'éboulis* (ébouler), *le hachis* (hacher), *le pâtis* (paître), *le taillis* (tailler), *le châssis* (enchâsser), *le cliquetis* (cliquer), *le coloris* (colorer), *le couchis* (coucher), *le logis* (loger), *le lattis* (latter). From a noun is derived *le palis* (G. pfahl, L. palum, Fr. pal).

§ 66. Lat. **(t)orius, a, um.**
Fr. **oir,** *masc.*; **oire,** *masc. and fem.*

From the nomina agentis in *tor* (*sor*) many derivatives are formed by the secondary suffix *ius, ia, ium*, signifying originally an instrument; as, *fac-tor-ium, e-munc-tor-ium*; but more frequently the place of the activity expressed by the verb. These words were originally adjectives, as is shown by the following forms: forum *Pistorium*, atrium *sutorium*, operculum *ambulatorium*. Very early, even in the classical period of the Latin language, the neuter forms of these adjectives were used as substantives: *quæstorium, prætorium, deversorium*. Their number was increased in the Silver Age: *auditorium, dormitorium, repositorium*; and continued to increase in Low Latin: *lusorium, consistorium, cenatorium, oratorium, repertorium, receptorium, lavatorium*. In Mediæval Latin we find *lectorium, refectorium, redemptorium, laboratorium, observatorium*. Of the feminine form only three substantives are formed: *vic-tor-ia, his-tor-ia* (connected with εἰδέναι, root ιδ, and G. *wiss-en*), and *gl-or-ia* (from *clu-ěre*, related to κλέ-ος). In *tect-orium, port-orium, tent-orium, pro-mont-orium*, we find *orium* treated like a simple suffix and appended to a nominal stem, showing that the original meaning of the compound suffix was gradually fading from the mind of the Latin-speaking population.

In French all those in *toir* and *toire* taken from Latin neuters in *torium* are masculines: *le purgatoire, le laboratoire, un oratoire, le prétoire, le réfectoire, un auditoire, un directoire, le monitoire, le dortoir* (dormitorium). In words of French formation the suffix *oir* is added to the stem of the verb: *un arrosoir* (arroser), *un semoir* (semer), *un comptoir* (compter), *un rasoir* (raser), *un accordoir* (accorder), *un miroir* (mirer), *un crachoir* (cracher), *un brunissoir* (brunir), *un abattoir* (abattre), *un parloir* (parler), *un lavoir* (laver), *un mouchoir* (moucher), *un trottoir* (trotter), *un laminoir* (laminer), *un chauffoir* (chauffer), *un abreuvoir* (abreuver), *un éteignoir* (éteindre), *un grattoir* (gratter), *un décussoire* (décusser). But feminines formed after this analogy are: *une balançoire* (balancer), *une bassinoire* (bassiner), *une décrottoire* (décrotter), *une écumoire* (écumer), *une lardoire* (larder), *une mâchoire* (mâcher), *une mangeoire* (manger), *une rôtissoire* (rôtir), *une écritoire* (which, however, cannot be derived from *écriv-ant*, but must be rather from *scriptorium*), and *une armoire* (armer, armarium).

From the feminine form in *oria* three substantives are derived: *la gloire, la victoire, une histoire.*

In a few instances, two nouns of different gender, and with a different meaning, are derived from the same verb:—

baigner	un baignoir, *a bathing place*	une baignoire, *a bathing tub*
fouler	un fouloir, *a rammer*	une fouloire, *a fulling board*
racler	un racloir, *a scraper*	une racloire, *a strickle, strike*

§ 67. Lat. **antia, entia,** *fem.*
Fr. **ance, ence,** *fem.*

A large number of abstract nouns are formed in Latin from the participle present by the suffix *ia*: *constant-ia, infant-ia* (fari), *scient-ia, provident-ia.* Most of these pass into French, those derived from verbs of the first conjugation naturally taking the termination *ance*, whilst those from the other three conjugations take *ence*: *constance, ignorance, enfance, jactance, audience, décence, innocence, prudence, providence, science, sentence.* Of the large number of modern words formed by this suffix, those in *ance* are derived from French participles present, whilst those in *ence* are from French adjectives or Latin participles: *suffisance* (suffisant), *naissance* (naissant), *confiance* (confiant), *obéissance* (obéissant), *croissance* (croissant), *surveillance* (surveillant), *défiance* (défiant), *usance* (usant), *vengeance* (vengeant), *croyance* (croyant), *alliance* (alliant); but *adhérence* (adhérent), *urgence* (urgent), *permanence* (permanent), *exigence* (exigens *not* exigeant), *cadence* (cadens).

§ 68. Lat. **(t)ura,** *fem.*
Fr. **ure,** *fem.*

The suffix *tura* (*sura*) qualifies the activity or expresses the result of the action of the verb to which it is appended. The majority of Latin nouns formed by it seem to be derivatives from the nomina agentis in *tor* (*sor*): *cultura, pictura, censura.*

But even in Latin the suffix *ura* is found added to the crude form of the verb : *fig-ura*. The majority of French words in *ure* are derived directly from the corresponding Latin words : *culture, nature, peinture, sculpture, censure, créature*. In words of French formation the suffix is appended to the stem of the verb, and in verbs of the second conjugation to the inchoative form : *allure, blessure, brûlure, doublure, dorure, parure, pâture* (paître), *salure, serrure, moisissure, flétrissure, bouffissure*. Rarely is this suffix appended to nominal stems : *droiture* (droit), *bouture* (bout), *verdure* (vert), *encolure* (col). *Bravoure* (brave) has modified the vowel of the suffix.

In accordance with the Latin formation are the following modern words : *aventure, ouverture, lecture, nourriture, bruniture*.

§ 69. Lat. **(tr)ina**, *fem.*
Fr. **ine**, *fem.*

This suffix has the same history as the preceding one. Originally, we find it used for the formation of feminines from nouns in *tor*, in order to express a place : *tex-tor, tex-tr-ina, pis-tor, pis-tr-ina, tons-(t)or, tons-tr-ina*; and afterwards abstract nouns : *doc-tor, doc-tr-ina*. But the suffix is likewise found attached to the verbal stem ; as, *ru-ina* (ruere), *far-ina* (ferre), *coqu-ina* (coquĕre). Most of these pass into French : *doctrine, ruine, farine, cuisine, discipline, saline*. Of French formation are *poitrine, racine* (from forms like *pectorina, racina*), *courtine, resine, colline, routine, saisine, gésine, famine, narine*. Frequent is this suffix in modern technical terms : *gélatine, fibrine, camelotine, cottonine, lustrine, quinine, vaccine* (vache), which, however, are all formed from nouns.

§ 70. Lat. **io** (gen. **ionis**), *fem.*
Fr. **ion**, *fem.*

The large number of abstract nouns formed by adding the suffix *io* to the verbal stem (*contag-io, leg-io, obliv-io, reg-io, relig-io, suspic-io*), or also to nominal stems (*commun-io, un-io, tal-io, rebell-io*), have passed without exception into French. Nevertheless, not one new word has been coined on French ground by this suffix. The normal French form is *ion*: *contagion, légion, opinion, rébellion, région, religion, communion*. *Soupçon* is a masculine formed from *soupçonner*. (See § 58.)

§ 71. Lat. **tio (sio)**, *fem.*
Fr. **tion, sion, son, çon**, *fem.*

Related to the preceding suffix is undoubtedly *tio (sio)*, of which we have spoken before (§ 26), and which is an enlarged form of the suffix *ti* : *men-ti-o* (mens, mentis). This suffix forms a considerable number of abstract nouns in Latin, which also have all passed into French. But, differing in this from *io*, it has preserved its formative power in French, chiefly in derivatives of the *a* and *i* conjugations. Of Latin origin are *action, motion, question, occasion, vision, procession, percussion, flexion, réflexion, génuflexion, fluxion, chanson* (cantionem), *raison* (rationem), *façon* (factionem), *leçon* (lectionem), *poison* (potionem), *maison* (mansionem), *toison* (tonsionem). Words formed in French with this suffix are *légalisation, certification, fanaison, fauchaison, floraison, livraison, garnison, guérison, boisson.*

§ 72. Lat. **nda**, *fem.* (of **ndus**).
Fr. **ande, ende**, *fem.*

From the Latin participle in *dus, a, um*, which is generally considered an enlarged form of the participle present, a few feminine substantives are derived ; but the suffix has become sterile in French : *une offrande, la reprimande, la viande* (vivenda), *la légende, la prébende, la provende* (providenda). The masculines *le multiplicande* and *le dividende* are explicable by the ellipsis of *numerus*. *L'ordinand,* as the name of a male person, has preserved a masculine termination.

§ 73. Lat. **ēla**, *fem.*
Fr. **elle, èle**, *fem.*

The small number of nouns formed by this suffix are also found in French. Analogous words have not been formed. *Chandelle* (candela), *corruptèle, clientèle, loquèle, tutelle* or *tutèle*.

Suffixes of Substantives derived from other Substantives.

As a large number of adjectives become substantives, even in Latin, and still more so in French, we shall find it best to treat among the suffixes forming substantives also those adjectival suffixes which in French have supplied a considerable number of substantives.

§ 74. Lat. **arius, a, um.**
Fr. **aire, ier.**

In Latin the suffixes *ari-s* and *ali-s* are identical. *Alis* forms adjectives from nominal stems containing an *r*, whilst *aris* is added to stems in *l*. Thus we have *rur-alis, mur-alis, austr-alis*; but *sol-aris, consul-aris, singul-aris*. Though identical in their origin, the subsequent history of these two suffixes diverges widely. From *aris* is formed an enlarged suffix, *arius, a, um*, which, with all its formative power, has passed into the Romance languages, whilst *alis* has never been enlarged in Latin, and has remained in the modern languages an almost barren suffix. From the time of Augustus the formations in *arius* increase rapidly and begin to be used as substantives. The force of this suffix is to name the agent (generally an artisan and trader) after the article he manufactures or deals in: *acuarius, coronarius, doliarius, annularius, carpentarius, candelabrarius*; or from the material in which he works or deals in: *aurarius, lapidarius, argentarius, marmorarius, plumbarius*; or from the tool with which he works: *cultrarius, lorarius, manicarius, parmularius*. The locality of action, the workshop, is expressed sometimes by the feminine, but more frequently by the neuter form: *ærarium, cibarium, armamentarium, ossuarium, plumbarium, pomarium, salarium, pulvinarium, argentaria, carbonaria, herbaria, vinaria, cretaria*.

So manifold are these forms in *arius*, that even our most complete dictionaries do not give all the forms found in the authors of the Silver Age, nor, when they give them, all their meanings. Curious is the enlargement of *arius* by reduplication; as, *sal-ari-arius pugill-ari-arius, calc-ari-arius, vin-ari-arius, ocul-ari-arius, ferr-ari-arius* and many others, which show the frequent use of the suffix.

Of the original suffix *aris*, only a few examples have been preserved in French: *écolier* (scholaris), *sanglier* (singularis, sc. aper), *oreiller* (auricularis), *luminaire* (luminar). On the other hand, the enlarged suffix *arius* has preserved in French all its original mobility of gender, meaning and formative power.

Names of persons in *aire* and *ier* from decidedly Latin forms are: *lapidaire, libraire, statuaire, argentier, chambrier* (camerarius), *huissier* (ostiarius), *écuyer* (scutarius), *conseillier* (consiliarius), *cavalier, chevalier*; whilst of unquestioned French formation are: *cessionnaire, diamantaire, propriétaire, banquier, pâtissier, usurier, jardinier, faïencier, menuisier* (minutus), *barbier, batelier, chamelier, cordier, geôlier, lanternier, potier, sellier, faisandier, bijoutier, cloutier, cafétier, chaînetier*; and, with absorption of the *i*: *berger* (vervecarius), *vacher* (vacca), *linger* (linge). Many of these substantives form a feminine; as, *la cessionaire, la batelière, la cafétière, la chambrière, la cordière, la lavandière, la fermière, la lingère, la bergère*.

Names of animals in *ier* : *bélier* (E. bell-wether), *le pluvier, le lévrier* (leporarius), *limier* (ligamen).

Names of plants derived from the name of the fruit: *amandier, cotonnier, cerisier, citronnier, cocotier, cacaotier, mûrier, câprier, églantier, fraisier, figuier, framboisier, poirier, pommier, prunier*; and, with the *i* absorbed : *noyer* (nucalis, nucarius). The following names of plants are, however, not derived from the name of the fruit: *laurier* (laurus), *peuplier* (populus).

A place or vessel containing anything is expressed by the following, which, as masculines, must be referred to the Latin *arium* : *colombier* (columbarium), *laraire* (lararium), *chartrier* (chartularium), *grenier* (granarium), *verger* (viridarium), *poulailler, baguier, encrier, huilier, poivrier, sablier, vinaigrier*; but also other derivatives, which express the object which bears or belongs to the thing expressed in the primitive word : *chandelier, échiquier, clocher, foyer, tablier, collier, oreillier, suaire* (sudarium), *calendrier* (calendarium), *annuaire, douaire*, (dotarium).

But, as in Latin, sometimes the feminine gender is preferred for these nouns: *aiguière, bonbonnière, coutelière, saucière, tabatière, théière, alunière, carrière, ratière, sablière, argentière, salière, tourbière, linière, crapaudière, filière, pépinière, barrière, tanière, boutonnière, litière, barrière, frontière* (frons), *fourmilière* (formicula), *rivière* (riparia), *crinière, prière* (precaria).

§ 75. Lat. **alis, ale.**
Fr. **al, el,** *masc.*

This suffix has been entirely displaced by the preceding one. Only a few remnants of it are to be found in the present language : *capital, hôtel* and *hôpital, local, canal, animal, fanal* (φανός), *madrigal* (mandra), *journal* (diurnalis), *signal, natal, noël* (natalis), *mistral* (magistralis), *duel* (dualis), *pluriel* (pluralis), *cardinal* (cardo, cardinalis), *ménestrel* (ministerialis), *caporal*. A few feminine adjectives in *ale* have become substantives : *la capitale* (sc. *ville*), *la pastorale* (sc. *chanson*).

The termination *lis* with preceding *i* has been preserved in *chenil* (canis), *fenil* (fœnile), *fusil* (focus), *campanile*.

§ 76. Lat. **anus, ana.**
Fr. **ain, en, an,** *masc.*; **aine, enne, ane,** *fem.*

A great many adjectives are formed in Latin by adding the suffix *anus* to nominal stems, especially to geographical names, which at a very early period began to be used substantively. In French the suffix has been rarely employed for the formation of substantives, and never been used sufficiently for attaining even uniformity of spelling. Thus we have in *ain* : *Africain, Alain, Germain, Romain, Syracusain, Napolituin, Palermitain* (Panormitanus), *Samaritain* ; and of modern origin : *Mexicain. Américain, Chartrain* (Chartres). From other than geographical names are : *aubain* (L. L. *albanus*, a foreigner, from *alibi*), *publicain* (publicanus), *châtelain* (castellanus), *chapelain* (capellanus), *écrivain.* Sometimes the suffix assumes the form *en* : *Chaldéen, Galiléen, Phocéen, Européen, Iduméen, Achéen, Vendéen, doyen* (decanus), *citoyen* (like civit-anus) ; occasionally the form *an* : *Pisan, Tolosan, Toscan, Mantouan, Parmesan, Padouan, Castillan, Catalan, vétéran, artisan, partisan, paysan, courtisan.* They form nearly all feminine substantives according to the general rules of descriptive grammar : *châtelaine, Romaine, citoyenne, courtisane.* A few feminines are formed in *aine* : *la fontaine* (fontana), *une aubaine* (*albana*, see above *aubain*), *la mitaine, la fredaine,* and the collective numerals : *huitaine, neuvaine, douzaine, vingtaine, trentaine,* with which must be classed *semaine* (septimana), and the metrical terms *quatrain, sixain, douzain.*

§ 77. Lat. **ianus, iana.**
Fr. **ien, ienne.**

The French suffix *ien* has served chiefly for forming the names of nations from the names of countries, and the names of persons from the name of their trade or occupation. Its use is far more extended than that of the corresponding Latin *ianus*. Thus, for instance, the greatest part of names of countries in *ia* presuppose a gentile noun or adjective in *us* ; as, *Lydia*, Lydus ; *Babylonia*, Babylonius ; *India*, Indus ; *Venetia*, Venetus ; or have variously formed gentile nouns as a base ; as, *Thracia*, Thrax ; *Caria*, Car ; *Phœnicia*, Phœnix and Phœnicius ; *Macedonia*, Macedo ; *Athenæ*, Atheniensis. All these various forms are absorbed in French by the suffix *ien* : *Lydien, Assyrien, Babylonien, Indien, Vénitien, Dorien, Béotien, Thracien, Phénicien, Macédonien, Athénien.* Modern gentile names follow this analogy : *Algérien, Alsacien, Artésien, Autrichien, Bohémien, Prussien, Norwégien, Parisien, Péruvien, Canadien, Languedocien.* Very large is the number of personal nouns, expressing trade or occupation, formed by this suffix : *pharmacien, gardien, physicien, opticien, magicien, chirurgien, comédien, musicien, grammairien, historien, théologien, mécanicien.* The suffix is further used for naming an individual from the society or sect he belongs to : *académicien, patricien, paroissien, chrétien, presbytérien, Luthérien, Socinien, Platonicien, Pythagoricien, Stoïcien, Epicurien.*

All these substantives are capable of forming feminine substantives or adjectives in *ienne*, with the exception of a few proper names like *Appien, Dioclétien, Gratien, Bastien.*

§ 78. Lat. **etum,** *neut.* (**eta**).
Fr. **aie,** *fem.*

A small number of substantives, having chiefly reference to rustic affairs, are formed by the suffix *etum* (aie), which denotes a place in which the thing named in the stem abounds: *jonchaie* (juncetum), *olivaie* (olivetum), *aunaie* (alnetum), *saussaie* (salicetum, salictum), *roseraie* (rosaretum, rosetum), *Fontenay* (Fontanetum), *Aulnay* (alnetum), *Chatenay* (Castanetum), *ronceraie, boulaie, chênaie, foutelaie.*

§ 79. L. Lat. **aticum, agium.**
Fr. **age,** *masc.*

In its last stage of decomposition the Low Latin produced a new suffix, *aticum, agium,* by which various shades of meaning were effected in nominal stems. Thus we find *herbaticum, herbagium* (herba), *coraticum, coragium* (cor), *formaticum, formagium* (forma), *viaticum, viagium* (via). Its French form *age* has proved one of the most productive and versatile suffixes in forming substantives not only from other substantives and verbs, but also from adjectives (*enfantillage,* infantilis; *parage,* par), and even from prepositions (*avantage,* avant = ab-ante; *outrage,* outre, ultra*). Generally speaking, it may be said that *age* intensifies the meaning of the base. As many words have different meanings, signifying at the same time an activity, or the result of that activity, a property or a condition, it is somewhat difficult to arrange the many derivatives formed by this suffix in distinct classes.

Collective nouns in *age* are: *branchage, feuillage, ramage, cordage, herbage, nuage, plumage, vitrage, verbiage, voisinage, rouage, paysage, pâturage.*

Closely allied to these are augmentatives like *marécage, ombrage, personnage, ouvrage, coquillage.*

A condition or property is expressed by *apprentissage, esclavage, courage, veuvage, parage.*

An intensified activity is expressed by *badinage, baladinage,*

---

* Although perhaps *outrer* was first formed from *ultra,* and *outrage* from *outrer.* The same doubt will arise in many other nouns formed by this suffix.

carnage, hommage, langage, orage (aura), *voyage* (via, viaticum), *pillage, pélérinage, flottage, brigandage*.

The activity, and sometimes the result of that activity, are expressed in *cabotage, filage, jardinage, labourage, blanchissage, abordage, outrage, passage, partage, racommodage, ravaudage, héritage, dommage, témoignage, éclairage, ménage* (perhaps *maisonnage*, mansionaticum, but more likely from *méner*, minare).*

But the various shades of meaning produced in the base by this suffix defy classification. Sometimes it means 'belonging to,' or 'contained in,' or 'arising from;' as, *fromage* (forma), *ermitage, visage, potage* (pot), *quaiage*.

Not to be confounded with this truly modern French suffix are words derived from the Latin in *ago*, which are of the feminine gender: *image* (imago), and *une plage* (plaga), *la rage* (rabies), *la page* (pagina), *la nage* (from *nager, navigare*).

§ 80. Lat. **atus**, *masc.*
Fr. **at, é,** *masc.*

The Latin suffix *atus* (gen. *ūs*: *episcopatus, consulatus*) in its Latin form *at* retains also its Latin meaning of 'office,' 'estate of': *cardinalat, célibat, épiscopat, patriciat, apostolat, diaconat, archidiaconat, électorat, vicariat, généralat*. In its more modern form *é* it expresses more commonly the territory subject to the dignitary expressed in the base: *comté, duché, évêché, Dauphiné, principauté*. But the termination *at* has remained with this meaning in *marquisat, landgraviat, palatinat*. Collective nouns are *clergé* and *sénat*.

§ 81. Lat. **ata**, *fem.*
Fr. **ade, ée,** *fem.*

Numerous are the derivatives formed from substantives by *ade* and *ée*. The former shows clearly the origin of this suffix to be the Latin *ata* (the feminine form of *atus*), which as a suffix occurs only in Mediæval Latin, so that both forms *ade* and *ée* may be considered suffixes of purely Romance formation. The various meanings of the suffix shade frequently off into one another. A compound formed by a collection of the things expressed in the base are named by *palissade, colonnade, barricade* (barrique), *balustrade, enfilade, estocade*. An intensified activity, and sometimes also the result

---

* *Minare*, to drive cattle by threats, a collateral form of *minari*, used by Appianus Marcellinus and Priscian. See Riddle and White, *s. v.*

of that activity, are expressed in *fusillade, cannonade, ballotade, bastonnade, dragonnade, ruade, tirade, cavalcade, gambade, estrapade*. The object which results from the base is expressed in *salade, estouffade, limonade, carbonnade, parade, brigade, estrade, exouade, charade.** *La caronade* (a species of ordnance) is so named after its place of manufacture, Carron, in Stirlingshire. In *passade* and *bourgade* the suffix has a diminutive sense. Still more frequent is the form *ée*, which must not be confounded with the feminine form of the past participle used substantively. (See § 56.) For although this suffix has its origin in a participial form, it is nevertheless used far more frequently for the formation of derivatives from substantives than from verbs. Its most ordinary meaning is that of the English *full* in compounds (*plateful*, etc.): *bouchée, brassée, charretée, chaudronnée, poignée, assiettée, batelée, becquée, cuillerée, cuvée, couvée, écuellée, gorgée, hottée, pellée, maisonnée, panerée, pellerée, platée, potée, tassée, ruée*. Time considered with regard to its duration is expressed by *année, matinée, soirée, veillée, journée*. Augmentatives or frequentatives are *nuée, bruée, risée, rosée, marée, guilée*. Something effected by the base is rarely expressed by this suffix: *hommée* (a plot of land which a man can cultivate in a day), *araignée* (cobweb), *denrée* (what can be bought for a denarius).

§ 82. Fr. **erie**, *fem.*

The suffix *erie* has its origin in the custom of the Romance languages of forming substantives from infinitives of the first conjugation by adding the suffix *ie* (*ia*): *tromper-ie, flatter-ie*. The use of the suffix *ie* is then extended to substantives ending in *er*: *boulanger-ie*; and then *erie* is used as a new formative suffix, and appended equally to nominal and to verbal stems for the formation of derivative substantives.

A strikingly similar process is observable in German, where the corresponding suffix *ei* forms abstract nouns from nouns in *er*: *färber-ei, jäger-ei, zauber-ei, bäcker-ei, meier-ei*. In course of time the suffix is appended to nouns whose plural ends in *er*: *kind-er-ei, länd-er-ei, büch-er-ei*, and then *erei* is used as a new suffix, and indiscriminately added to verbs and nouns for the formation of new derivatives: *ras-erei, zier-erei, schwein-erei, büb-erei, sclav-erei*. But we must beware of inferring that the German suffix *erei* had any influence on the

---

* *Charade*, either from *carrus, carricata*, a cart-load; or from Ital. *ciarlare*, to chatter, to prate, from which are derived *ciarlatano*, a quack, and *ciarlataneria*, quackery.

development of the French suffix *erie*, or the reverse. The two languages formed two suffixes of striking resemblance by strikingly similar processes, but quite independently of one another.

The most ordinary force of *erie* is to form abstract nouns expressing an activity, which by usage mostly pass into nouns expressing a property. Thus *brusquerie* means abruptness, and, as a repeated act of abruptness, gruffness. In many cases *erie* is used for the formation of words expressing an office, trade, art, or occupation, which words are then used also for naming the place where such trade, art, or occupation is carried on, and not unfrequently in a third meaning, expressing the result or object of such trade or activity. Thus *charpenterie* means the art or trade of a carpenter, a carpenter's yard, and a carpenter's or timber work. *La boucherie* means the trade of a butcher, a butcher's shop, a slaughter-house, and, figuratively, it expresses indiscriminate slaughter. *Friperie* means trade in old clothes, an old clothes' shop, and old clothes as well themselves. There is not a single word in the subjoined lists which is not used in two or more of these meanings.

An act, frequently implying that the act is censurable, and hence a quality or property, is expressed by *espiéglerie, brusquerie, bouderie, fâcherie, étourderie, singerie, badauderie, niaiserie, bégueulerie, bigoterie, cachotterie, causerie, criaillerie, clabauderie, chicanerie, menterie, hâblerie, diablerie, flatterie, gagerie, tromperie, lorgnerie, ivrognerie, gloutonnerie, fourberie, agacerie, minauderie, philosopherie, poltronnerie, tricherie.*

A place is expressed by *bergerie, boucherie, ménagerie, lingerie, boulangerie, fruiterie, bouverie, canarderie, faisanderie, ladrerie, juiverie, hôtellerie, laiterie, huilerie, huisserie* (doorframe, from *ostium*), *affinerie, briqueterie, chancellerie, galerie, nourricerie.*

Trade or occupation, with other meanings flowing immediately from it, is expressed by *sorcellerie, piraterie, pénitencerie, oiselerie, charpenterie, commanderie, cristallerie, pâtisserie, ébénisterie, charlatanerie, marbrerie, mégisserie, friperie, herberie, pelleterie, plomberie.*

To those in the preceding lists, which also name a product, the following may be added: *argenterie, bijouterie, broderie, maçonnerie, soierie, verrerie, sucrerie, droguerie, verroterie, boiserie.*

As collectives may be considered: *infanterie, artillerie, loterie, cavallerie, tapisserie, messagerie*

§ 83. Lat. **ista**, *masc.*
Fr. **iṣte**, *masc.*

In patristic Latin a suffix *ista*, formed from the Greek ιστής (κιθαριστής), was used for the formation of nomina agentis: *baptista, evangelista, psalmista*. Its use has been somewhat extended in French, inasmuch as it serves not only to signify a man who cultivates a certain science or art, but also such as follow a certain doctrine: *anatomiste, allégoriste, fabuliste, organiste, naturaliste, chimiste, oculiste, artiste, évangéliste, annaliste, dentiste, droguiste, ébéniste, herboriste, latiniste, paysagiste, pianiste, duelliste, monarchiste, royaliste, communiste, matérialiste, socialiste, papiste, moraliste, fataliste.*

§ 84. Lat. **ismus**, *masc.*
Fr. **isme**, *masc.*

The Greek suffix ισμός was introduced into the Latin language by grammarians in the classical period, for the formation of technical terms: *barbarismus, solœcismus, archaismus, syllogismus*. In French its use has remained the same: *paganisme, mahométisme, christianisme, athéisme, mécanisme, fanatisme, héroïsme, Mosaïsme, Aristotélisme, Platonisme, atomisme, anglicisme, gallicisme, communisme, idéalisme, socialisme, égoïsme, mutisme*. From the Greek ισμα are *le prisme, le schisme*.

SUFFIXES OF SUBSTANTIVES DERIVED FROM ADJECTIVES.

§ 85. The Latin suffixes, used for the formation of substantives from adjectives, are *tas, tia, ia* and *tudo*. They are found in French in the numerous derivatives, which were received ready-made into the language. But *tas, tia* and *ia* have been productive of many modern derivatives, whilst *tudo* has been used only in the formation of three or four new words.

All substantives derived from adjectives are of the feminine gender both in the Latin and French languages.

§ 86. Lat. **tas**.
Fr. **té**.

The most usual suffix of this class is *tas*, which in Latin is rarely added without the connecting vowel *e* or *i* (*atroci-tas, pi-e-tas*). As bases serve chiefly adjectives but frequently also substantives (*tempestas, virginitas, civitas, venustas*), rarely verbs (*egestas, potestas, voluntas*). By far the largest number of French words in *té* follow Latin derivatives in *tas*: *activité, agilité, assiduité, atrocité, célérité, facilité, fatuité, morosité, perspicuité, rusticité, stabilité, verbosité, simplicité, obscurité, parité, amabilité, mortalité, variété, vérité, satiété*. Nouns formed according to this analogy add the suffix to the feminine form of the adjective, but fluctuate in the use of the connecting vowel. Those of more recent and popular origin seem to prefer *e*: *netteté, saleté, souveraineté, fausseté, fermeté, naïveté, honnêteté, légèreté, pauvreté, gaieté, suzeraineté, acariâtreté*; whilst *i* is not uncommon, especially in derivatives from adjectives in *eux, euse*: *porosité* (poreux), *monstruosité*, (monstrueux), *frivolité, légitimité, nullité, nudité, priorité, supériorité*. Bases ending in a liquid frequently reject the connecting vowel both in Latin and French: *faculté* (facultas), *difficulté* (difficultas), *liberté* (libertas), *volonté* (voluntas), which practice is still further extended in French: *clarté* (clar-i-tas), *santé* (san-i-tas). Amongst these we ought to reckon those in *l* which vocalize this consonant: *beauté* (bellus), *cruauté* (crudelitas).

§ 87. Lat. **ia**.
Fr. **ie**.

Added to adjective bases *ia* forms abstract nouns expressing qualities (*miser-ia*); added to the bases of nomina gentilia it forms names of countries (*Ital-ia*). Both are done by *ie* in French. But the Greek suffixes εια and ία (δημοκρατία, ἀριστοκράτεια) have exercised a decided influence on the French suffix, although the number of words formed analogous to the Greek, and not taken directly from the Greek, is very small. Latin forms are: *argutie, facétie, inertie, ineptie, minutie, modestie, patrie, perfidie*; and of countries: *Arabie, Arcadie, Asie, Arménie, Assyrie, Béotie, Germanie, Helvétie, Ligurie, Lusitanie, Laconie, Mysie, Samarie, Pannonie, Phénicie, Thessalie*. French forms are: *courtoisie, jalousie, maladie*; rarely derived from substantives: *clergie* (clerc), *compagnie* (compagne), *Normandie, Cafrerie, Dalécarlie, Picardie, Lettonie, Laponie, Valaquie, Turquie, Tartarie, Franconie*. Greek forms are: *démocratie, aristocratie, chimie*, in imitation of which we have *géologie, biographie, hydrophobie, anomalie, astronomie, géographie, archéologie, minéralogie*.

The Latin suffix *ia* is represented in French by final *e* when the word retains its original Latin accent: *angoisse* (angustia), *audace* (audacia), *concorde* (concordia), *envie* (invidia), *grâce* (gratia), *milice* (militia), *misère* (miseria); and in names of countries, especially of those ending in *onia, ania*, and *annia*: *Bretagne* (Britannia), *Espagne* (Hispania), *Champagne*

(Campania), *Romagne* (Romania), *Allemagne* (Allemannia), *Catalogne* (Catalonia), *Gascogne* (Vasconia), *Pologne* (Polonia), *Cologne* (Colonia), *Boulogne* (Bononia), *Sardaigne* (Sardinia), *Prusse* (Borussia), *Grèce* (Græcia), *Inde* (India), *Gaule* (Gallia), *Alsace, Provence, Suède, Thrace, Perse.*

§ 88. Lat. **it-ia, itia.**
Fr. **ice, ise, esse.**

The Latin suffix *itia* (which generally coincides with *ities*) cannot in French be distinguished from words in *ia* derived from a base ending in *t* (*inept-ia*). The French form *ice* appears most frequently in words taken ready-made from the Latin : *avarice* (avaritia), *immondice* (immunditia, -ies), *justice* (justitia), *notice* (notitia). The form *ise* is more peculiar to words of French formation : *accortise* (accort), *balourdise* (balourd), *bâtardise* (bâtard), *bêtise* (bête), *convoitise* (concupisc-), *franchise* (franc), *friandise* (friand), *gaillardise* (gaillard), *lourdise* (lourd), *marchandise* (marchand), *sottise* (sot). The form *esse* frequently represents the Latin *itia*, but is by far the most usual suffix for the formation of new nouns : *justesse* (justitia), *mollesse* (mollitia), *paresse* (pigritia), *tristesse* (tristitia) ; and of French formation : *aînesse* (aîné), *altesse* (alt-us, haut), *finesse* (fin), *hardiesse* (hardi), *ivresse* (ivre), *jeunesse* (jeune), *largesse* (largus), *noblesse* (noble), *politesse* (poli), *richesse* (riche), *sagesse* (sage), *tendresse* (tendre), *vieillesse* (vieil), *vitesse* (vite), *sécheresse* (sec), *faiblesse* (faible), *bassesse* (bas), *délicatesse* (délicat), *petitesse* (petit), *adresse* (addirectus).

§ 89. Lat. **tudo.**
Fr. **tude.**

The suffix *tudo* had nearly lost its formative power in the classical period of the Latin language. Many derivatives were formed by it, chiefly from adjectives in the ante-classical period, which classical writers displace by derivatives in *tas*. Thus we find as archaic expressions, especially in the scenic poets : *anxitudo, claritudo, castitudo, celebritudo, duritudo, firmitudo, gracilitudo, hilaritudo, honestudo, lenitudo, suavitudo, sævitudo, severitudo, sanctitudo, temeritudo, vanitudo, vastitudo,* for which Classical Latin has the forms *anxietas, claritas, castitas, celebritas, duritas, firmitas, gracilitas, hilaritas, honestas, lenitas, suavitas, sævitas, severitas, sanctitas, temeritas, vanitas, vastitas.* The forms in *ies* (*durities*) and *do* (*dulcedo*) likewise assist in displacing the older suffix, without, however, striking as deep roots into the language as the suffix *tas*. From this it is plain that the suffix *tudo* would not be used in French for the formation of many new words. The only new formations are: *platitude* (plat), *promptitude* (prompt), *certitude* (certus), *exactitude* (exactus), *gratitude* (gratus). All the rest are from Latin words which have resisted the absorbing power of *tas*: *altitude, amplitude, aptitude, attitude* (aptitudo), *béatitude, desuétude, habitude, lassitude, latitude, longitude, mansuétude, multitude, servitude, similitude, sollicitude, turpitude, vicissitude, plénitude, inquiétude, solitude*. By rejection of the *d* and attraction of the suffix of the accusative, we have *amertume* (amaritudinem), and *coûtume* (consuetudinem).

Suffixes of Diminutives and Augmentatives.

§ 90. The Romance languages are rich in suffixes for the formation of augmentatives, diminutives, depreciatives, and the like. These suffixes are partly of Latin (*ulus, a, um*; *culus, a, um*; *inus, a, um*; *aceus, a, um*; *aster*), partly of German origin (*ard, arde*; *aud, aude*). Others again are pure Romance suffixes (*at, ate*; *et, ette*; *ot, otte*). The frequent use of diminutival suffixes occasionally weakens their force; thus we have, even in Latin, words in which no Roman would have recognised a diminutive, like *pop-ulus, speculum*. Nevertheless, by the very same suffix Modern French has formed *molécule*, which has both the appearance and force of a diminutive. The force of the suffix was especially weakened in words which were received ready-formed from Latin or German; as, *cheville* (clavicula), *formule* (formula); whilst in those formed in French the suffix retains its force. In a few instances augmentatives or diminutives seem to have been formed, because, after the rejection of the Latin suffix, a word remained which to the Romance ear appeared too short. Thus *abeille* (apis, apicula), *oreille* (auris, auricula), *soleil* (sol, soliculus), *taureau* (taurus, taurellus), *rognon* (ren), though diminutives in form, express no more than their simple Latin bases. Very common is the addition of two of these suffixes (*corps, cors-et, cors-el-et*; *agn-eau, agn el-et*; *Pierre, Perr-in, Perr-in-et*; *Marie, Mari-on, Mar-ion-ette*), which was also frequently done in Latin (*cista, cistella, cistellula*; *puer, puella*, instead of *puerula, puellula*). The following are the most ordinary of these suffixes, with their most usual combinations:—

Latin Suffixes.

§ 91. **ulus, a, um** (ule, *m.* and *f.*). Nouns in which the diminutive meaning has been lost, throw out *u* when a consonant precedes it: *peuple* (populus), *sauge* (cingulum), *seille* (situla), *table* (tabula), *tuile* (tegula). Words which remain diminutives preserve also their original Latin form: *le capitule* (capitulum), *le conciliabule* (conciliabulum), *le globule* (globulus), *le module* (modulus), *la formule* (formula), *la canule* (cannula), *la capsule* (capsula), *la cellule* (cellula), *la fécule* (fæcula), *la glandule* (glandula), *la pilule* (pilula), *la plantule* (plantula), *lunule, virgule, plumule*. *Le pendule* (pendulum), *la pendule* (pendula). Those in *ole*, as *girandole, gondole*, have passed through the Italian.

culus, a, um (cule, *m.* and *f.*) is a very frequent suffix, and must be considered according to the letter which precedes it.

culus preceded by a consonant has been preserved in a few words: *oncle* (avunculus), *escarboncle* (carbunculus), *muscle* (musculus), *cercle* (circulus), *couvercle* (operculum). Larger is the number of recently imported words: *animalcule, corpuscule, opercule, opuscule, caroncule, portioncule*.

a-culus, a, um: *gouvernail* (gubernaculum), *soupirail* (suspirare = suspiraculum), *éventail* (eventilare), *graille (gracula* instead of *graculus*), *tenaille* (tenaculum). Of modern formation are: *épouvantail, fermail, plumail, travail, sonnaille*.

e-culus, a, um; i-culus, a, um: *orteil* (articulus), *soleil* (sol-iculus), *sommeil* (somn-iculus), *péril* (periculum), *abeille* (apicula), *oreille* (auricula), *bouteille* (M. L. buticula), *corbeille* (corbicula), *corneille* (cornicula), *cheville* (clavicula), *goupil* (vulpecula), *ouaille* (ovicula), *essieu* (axiculus), *croustille* (crusta), *lentille* (lenticula), *coutille* (culter). According to analogy are formed: *groseille, chenille, jonquille, pointille, oseille* (ὀξάλιος).

u-culus, a, um: *fenouil* (fœn(i)uculum), *verrou* (verr(i)-uculum), *genou* (gen(i)uculum), *grenouille* (rana).

Many modern words which preserve more closely their Latin form have been introduced. Masculines: *follicule, indicule, monticule, pédicule, réticule*. Feminines: *auricule, canicule, clavicule, cuticule, lenticule, particule, pellicule, radicule, silicule, molécule, nubécule*. A change of gender has taken place in *une utricule* (utriculus).

From the Latin **aceus, iceus (icius), oceus**, a suffix is formed which generally expresses degeneration or enlargement. It appears in the various forms of *as* (aceus), *asse, ace, ache* (acea), *iche, isse* (icea, icia), *oche* (ocea), *uche* (ucea). For those in *is* (icius), see § 65

Embarras (barre), *coutelas* (culter, cultellaceus?), *échalas* (scala), *tracas* (trac), *fatras* (fartum), *plâtras* (emplastum);

bécasse (bec), *crevasse* (crever), *cuirasse* (cuir), *paillasse* (paille), *paperasse* (papier), *bestiasse, laidasse, coignasse, tirasse, liasse; grimace, populace, rosace, villace, galéace; mordache, moustache, panache, rondache*; *levriche, pouliche, caniche; caboche, bamboche, galoche, mailloche, sacoche, filoche, épinoche.* Of the few in *uche*, a diminutive meaning is attached only to *guenuche* (petit guenon). In *peluche* (pellis), *breluche*, the meaning seems to be rather collective.

In Low Latin the suffix *ulus* was gradually displaced by *ellus* and *illus*. In words of Latin formation the suffix has rarely retained its diminutive force: *anneau* (*annellus* instead of *annulus*), *cerveau, flambeau, passereau, moineau, bâteau, bandeau, barreau, château, drapeau, fabliau, troupeau, écriteau, fourneau, fourreau, marteau, museau, poteau* (postis), *tuyeau* (O. N. tûda), *écuelle* (scutella), *hirondelle, sauterelle.* In modern formations this suffix has diminutive power, and is frequently added to the names of animals in order to denote the young : *chèvre, chevreau; pigeon, pigeonneau; dindon, dindonneau; faisan, faisandeau; paon, paonneau; saumon, saumonneau; renard, renardeau; lion, lionceau; tourtre, tourtereau; baleine, baleineau*; and sometimes as a secondary diminutive suffix after *et*: *levreteau, louveteau, cailleteau.* Diminutives of trees, of human beings, and even of inanimate things, are frequently formed by *eau*: *agneau, ormeau, chêneau, arbrisseau, préau, poétereau, larronneau, friponneau, pastoureau, faisceau* (fasciculus), *monceau* (monticellus), *pinceau, jouvenceau, damoiseau, oiseau* (avicella), *vaisseau* (vascellum).

lia. Several adjectives in *alis, ĭlis, īlis,* and *bilis,* are used substantively in Low Latin in their neuter plural form, which was considered a collective noun. Such substantives are *batualia, mortualia, genitalia, muralia, victualia, volatilia, mirabilia, nugalia.* From these were formed the French substantives in *aille*: *canaille* (canis), *racaille* (E. rack, wreck), *garçaille, moutonnaille, moinaille, gueusaille, truandaille, valetaille, rimaille, poissonnaille, tripaille, limaille, volaille, muraille, bataille, semaille, antiquaille, broussaille, entrailles, ferraille, fiançailles, quincaille, marmaille.* In a similar manner are to be explained the suffixes of *ormille, merveille, poitrail, bétail, portail, vitrail, béatilles, broutilles.* In many instances it will be difficult to determine with certainty whether those in *aille* follow a Latin form in *aculus, a, um,* or in *alia.*

The suffix *o* (*io*), French *on* (*ion*), was used in Latin for the formation of substantives signifying persons, animals, and things generally, e. g. *latro, prædo, falco, leo, carbo, mucro.*

In French this use of the suffix is continued, but it is fur her used as an augmentative and diminutive suffix; as which it is sometimes merely added to the base, but more frequently with the intervention of another diminutive suffix, particularly *ill, er, el,* and *et.*

Personalia formed by *on,* according to Latin precedent, from the occupation of the person, are: *larron, piéton, forgeron, bucheron, vigneron, poltron, espion, fripon.* The names of animals: *cochon, paon, pigeon, mouton, hérisson, poisson, limaçon;* direct from the Latin are *lion, scorpion, faucon.* Names of inanimate things are formed by this suffix according to analogy: *canton, charbon, houblon, flacon, jambon, menton, perron, manchon.* In some names of persons the suffix has depreciative power: *biberon, grognon, grison, glouton.*

As a diminutive, without a connecting suffix, it is used in: *aiglon, chaton, levron, oison, ourson, ânon, raton, carafon, cruchon, lanternon, sablon;* and frequently in proper names of women: *Fanchon* (Françoise), *Michon* (Michel), *Julion, Marion, Louison, Jeanneton, Margoton, Nanon, Ninon;* also in family names: *Ancillon, Gillon, Mabillon, Massillon.*

With the addition of a connecting diminutive suffix are formed: *bouvillon, négrillon, taurillon, carpillon, oisillon, brocheton, moucheron, clocheton, feuilleton.*

The Latin suffix *inus, a, um,* which originally was used only for the formation of adjectives from substantives (*asininus, caninus, cervinus, marinus*), is used in French also for the formation of substantives: *sapin, lapin, moulin, coussin, échevin, fantassin, jardin, famine, routine, narine, poitrine.* (Comp. § 69.) As a diminutive it is used in *Colin* (Colas), *Jupin* (Jupiter), *Perrin* (Pierre), *Robin* (Robert), *diablotin, culottin, pulverin;* and with the concomitant idea of the contemptible, in *faquin, coquin, dandin, galantin, poupin, catin* (f.). The German suffix *chen* is traceable in *mannequin, brodequin, lambrequin,* and perhaps in *arlequin.*

The Latin diminutive *aster* (*poetaster, filiaster, oleaster, pinaster, calvaster*) has survived only in a few Modern French substantives: *marâtre, parâtre, écolâtre, gentillâtre, mulâtre;* more frequently in adjectives: *bleuâtre, grisâtre, noirâtre, rougeâtre, bellâtre.**

* The necessity of making the largest possible lists of words derived by the same process, is shown by this rare suffix. *Ménage* explains *marâtre* to mean *mater atra.* This leaves the *s,* or circumflex accent, which regularly appears in the termination *âtre (astre)* to be accounted for, and the attempt to explain the rest of these derivatives in this manner, ends in absurdity.

German Suffixes.

§ 92. The German suffix *hart* was used in Old High German chiefly for the formation of nomina personalia: *Eberhart, Meinhart, Reinhart, Deganhart.* In Middle High German (and English) it is also used for appellativa; e. g. M. H. G. *nîthart, lüghart;* E. *drunkard, tankard, coward, bastard.* The force of the suffix is that of an augmentative, occasionally of a depreciative. In French, the number of substantives and adjectives formed by *ard* is very large. A considerable number of them are derived from verbal stems: *bavard* (baver), *babillard* (babiller), *braillard* (brailler), *criard* (crier), *fuyard* (fuir), *grognard* (grogner), *pendard* (pendre), *pillard* (piller). Others are from nominal bases: *bâtard* (bât), *béquillard* (béquille), *cagnard* (canis), *couard* (cauda),* *gueulard* (gueule), *mouflard* (moufle), *mouchard* (mouche), *soudard* (solde), *vieillard* (vieil), *montagnard* (montagne), *billard* (bille), *brassard* (bras), *cuissard* (cuisse), *mignard* (G. minne, *love*), *hagard*,† *blafard.* According to German precedent, a large number of personalia are formed in *ard* and *art*: *Bernard, Bayard, Blanchard, Erard, Regnard, Ronsard, Sicard, Havard, Abeillard, Béjard, Béjart, Gambart, Giffart,* to which may be added *Savoyard.* Names of animals: *canard, chevrillard, renard, beccard* (-*de*, f.), *grisard.* Names of things: *brancard, étendard, pétard, poignard, brocard, flambart.* Feminines are: *la moutarde* (mustum), *la nasarde* (nasus), *la mansarde* (Mansard, *nom. prop.*).

The German suffix *ald* (*vald*) seems, like the preceding one, to have been used originally for the formation of proper names, a large number of which survive to this day in Lombardy: *Garibaldi* (Weribald), *Grimaldi, Bertaldi, Rinaldo.* In French the suffix, with vocalised *l*, is appended both to verbal and adjectival bases: *badaud, bagaud, courtaud, finaud, lourdaud, nigaud, ribaud, rougeaud, suligaud, richaud, clabaud, pataud, crapaud, herbaut, levraut, héraut.* The number of these words was by far larger in Old French. Numerous are the family names: *Arnauld, Arnault, Marivault, Brunault, Bonald, Ferrault, Michault, Regnault, Rigault, Hunauld, Pinault.* To these must be reckoned *Saint-Cloud* (Chlodowald).

---

* Ital. *codardo*, one who turns tail.
† *Hagard*, generally derived from O. E. *hauke*, M. E. *hawk*. But it is more likely that the E. subst. *haggard* is from *hawk*, and that the adj. is to be brought into connection with E. *hag*, G. *hager, hexe*, &c.

French Suffixes.

§ 93. The three suffixes *at, et, ot,* m.; or *ate, ette, otte,* f., are peculiar to the Romance languages. They have been derived by some from the Celtic diminutive suffixes *that, nat, net, nit*; by others from the Germanic suffixes *aht, eht, iht, oht*. Their great antiquity is proved by the Lex Salica: ' Si quis *capritum* sive capram furatus fuerit.' Owing to their antiquity, these suffixes have lost their force in some derivatives of comparatively early formation.

The suffix *at* has been preserved in Modern French only in *goujat* and *verrat*. In Old French it was used more frequently: *aiglat, louvat*. This suffix must not be confounded with participial derivatives such as *opiat, forçat, miellat*.

By far the most frequent of these three suffixes is *et, ette*: *barillet, bassinet, cochet, jardinet, livret, poulet, rouet, sachet, loquet, navet, bouquet, ceinturette, chaussette, chemisette, chansonnette, fillette, historiette, maisonnette, manchette, villette, alouette, corvette, sornette, levrette*. Very frequently this suffix is used for the formation of diminutives from personal names: *Michelet, Jacquet, Blanchet, Condorcet, Annette, Antoinette, Georgette, Juliette, Louisette*. Often *et* appears as a secondary diminutive suffix: *archelet, agnelet, annelet, châtelet, corselet, sachelet, femmelette, tartelette, Perrinet*. The suffix has lost its diminutive force in *bouquet, bracelet, couplet, navet, valet, loquet, cliquette, lorgnette, lunette, anisette*.

Ot, otte has also lost its diminutive force in *cachot, abricot, mulot, javelot, capote, linotte*; and in many family names: *Abbot, Amelot, Brissot, Guiot, Petitot, Perrot, Oudinot, Marot, Clicquot*. In Christian names, on the other hand, it has preserved its diminutive force: *Margot, Pierrot, Charlot, Henriot, Jacot, Charlotte*, and in *îlot, hachot, bergerot*. In a few rare cases this suffix has the force of an augmentative, as in *ballot, gelinotte*.

OF THE ADJECTIVE.

§ 94. The loss of the neuter class of substantives entailed as a necessary consequence the loss of a separate neuter form for the adjective. The neuter form is grammatically only preserved in the substantive use of the adjective, as *le beau*.

The majority of Latin adjectives ending in *us, a, um,* the normal form for the two genders of French adjectives, corresponds to *us, a*: *bon* (bonus), *bonne* (bona), *vain* (vanus), *vaine* (vana).

§ 95. Nevertheless, some Latin adjectives in *us, a, um*, become in French adjectives of one termination: (*a*) those in *idus, a, um* (*rapide, cupide, avide*); (*b*) those in *arius, a, um* (*contraire, littéraire, primaire**); (*c*) those in *orius, a, um* (*méritoire, oratoire*); (*d*) those in *icus, a, um* (*classique, rustique, aulique*); (*e*) those in *imus, a, um* (*maritime, légitime, sublime, douzième, trentième*, etc.); (*f*) those which after throwing off the Latin suffix take for the sake of euphony a mute final *e* (*ferme, ample, digne, fixe, vaste, superbe, ronde*).

The small number of Latin adjectives in *er, a, um*, which are preserved in French, are adjectives of one termination: *pauvre, tendre, âpre, libre, sinistre, dextre*.

Adjectives in *er, is, e*, become in French adjectives of one termination: *aigre* (acer, cris, cre), *champêtre, sylvestre, célèbre, salubre, pédestre, équestre*.

All Latin adjectives in *is, e*, were originally in French adjectives of one termination. In Modern French a great many of these have gradually become adjectives of two terminations: *doux, douce* (dulcis, e), *fort, forte* (fortis, e), *grand, grande* (grandis, e), *bref, brève* (brevis, e); and particularly those in *alis*: *tel, telle* (talis, e), *quel, quelle* (quàlis, e), *fatal, fatale* (fatalis, e), *mortel, mortelle* (mortalis, e). The majority, however, have remained in Modern French adjectives of one termination: *triste, utile, aimable, fidèle*.

§ 96. In Old French all Latin adjectives of two terminations had but one termination for the two genders: *un homs loials, une fame loials*; *des ordres royalx, des lettres royalx*. Amongst the adjectives of this class which have passed and are passing into the class of adjectives of two terminations, some traces of this uniform termination may still be discovered. Thus the adjective *grand* has remained uniform in *grand'mère, grand'-messe, grand'route, grand'rue, grand'tante*, where the apostrophe has been put in later times for a mute *e*, which has been supposed to have been thrown out. So far from this being the case, this adjective seems even in these combinations to be assuming a separate form for the feminine, as the more modern mode of spelling in *grande messe, grande rue*, clearly proves. Another remnant of this formation is preserved in the rule that the participle present, when used adjectively, is invariable as long as it retains the full meaning of the verb and expresses

---

* But also *premier, première*.

an action and not a quality. But even this participle is frequently treated like an adjective of two terminations: *Le goût, la rime, en poésie, l'harmonie, les figures décident*, says Aubertin.*

§ 97. Latin adjectives of one termination are also in French adjectives of common gender (*féroce, vorace*). But all those from original participles present pass into the class of adjectives of two terminations: *plaisant, plaisante* (placentem), *ardent, ardente* (ardentem).

§ 98. The declension of adjectives is like that of substantives. The Old French declension of adjectives followed more closely the Latin declension:—

	Masc.	Fem.
Nom. Sing.	bons (bonus)	bone (bona)
Cas. Obl.	bon (bonum)	bone (bonam)
Nom. Plur.	bon (boni)	bones (bonæ)
Cas. Obl.	bons (bonos)	bones (bonas)

And for adjectives of one termination:—

Nom. Sing.	temporels
Cas. Obl.	temporel
Nom. Plur.	temporel
Cas. Obl.	temporels

§ 99. The formation of the plural of adjectives in *al* is not settled. The Académie observes a discreet silence in the case of many doubtful words. The general rule is to form the plural in *aux*. But the Old French form *als* is preserved in *amicals, fatals, finals, frugals, glacials, initials, labials, linguals, matinals, médials, natals, navals, ovals, pascals, pénals, théâtrals, virginals, vocals*. French grammarians and authors use these adjectives in *al* with a somewhat ludicrous timidity, and recommend, as the safest rule, to avoid using them in the masculine plural, and to say, for instance, instead of *combats navals, combats de mer*; or, instead of *les Allemands sont musicaux* (George Sand), to say, *les Allemands ont beaucoup de talent pour la musique*. The plurals especially to be avoided are those of *austral, boréal, canonial, conjugal, fatal, filial, final, frugal, jovial, pastoral, nasal, total, spécial, nuptial, pectoral*, and others. But of the majority of these words plurals may be found, in good authors, both in *als* and *aux*. Many of them are of rare occurrence, and have scarcely become naturalised in French.†

* See on this subject, Jullien, *Traité de Grammaire Française*, and Aubertin, *Grammaire moderne des Écrivains Français*.

† This pedantry has supplied Boursault with the material for an amusing scene in his 'Le Mercure Galant' (act iv. scene 7):—

ADJECTIVES.

§ 100. The comparative of adjectives was formed in Latin by the suffix *ior, ius,* and the superlative by *issimus, a, um.* In the case of adjectives whose crude form ends in a vowel, the Romans, for the sake of euphony, used the adverb *magis*

La Rissole.

. . . . . .
Vous saurez que toujours je fus homme de guerre,
Et brave sur la mer autant que sur la terre.
J'étais sur un vaisseau quand Ruyter fut tué,
Et j'ai même à sa mort le plus contribué :
Je fus chercher le feu que l'on mit à l'amorce
Du canon qui lui fit rendre l'âme par force.
Lui mort, les Hollandais suffrirent bien des *mals* !
On fit couler à fond les deux vice-*amirals*.

Merlin.

Il faut dire des *maux, vice-amiraux.* C'est l'ordre.

La Rissole.

Les *vice-amiraux* donc ne pouvant plus nous mordre,
Nos coups aux ennemis furent des coups *fataux* ;
Nous gagnâmes sur eux quatre combats *navaux*——

Merlin.

Il faut dire *fatals* et *navals.* C'est la règle.

La Rissole.

Les Hollandais réduits à du biscuit de seigle,
Ayant connu qu'en nombre ils étaient *inégals,*
Firent prendre la fuite aux vaisseaux *principals*——

Merlin.

Il faut dire *inégaux, principaux.* C'est le terme.

La Rissole.

Enfin, après cela nous fûmes à Palerme.
Les bourgeois à l'envi nous firent des *régaux* :
Les huit jours qu'on y fut furent huit *carnavaux.*

Merlin.

Il faut dire *régals* et *carnavals.*

La Rissole.

Oh ! dame,
M'interrompre à tous coups, c'est me chiffonner l'âme
Franchement.

Merlin.

Parlez bien. On ne dit point *navaux,*
Ni *fataux,* ni *régaux,* non plus que *carnavaux.*
Vouloir parler ainsi, c'est faire une sottise.

for the comparative, and *maxime* for the superlative. In the decay of the Latin inflections, the Romance languages adopted

La Rissole.

Eh, mordié! Comment donc voulez-vous que je dise?
Si vous me reprenez lorsque je dis des *mals*,
Inégals, principals, et des vice-*amirals*,
Lorsqu'un moment après, pour mieux me faire entendre,
Je dis *fataux, navaux*, devez-vous me reprendre?
J'enrage de bon cœur quand je trouve un trigaud,
Qui souffle tout ensemble et le froid et le chaud.

Merlin.

J'ai la raison pour moi qui me fait vous reprendre,
Et je vais clairement vous le faire comprendre.
Al est un singulier dont le pluriel fait *aux*.
On dit, 'C'est mon *égal*,' et 'Ce sont mes *égaux*.'
C'est l'usage.

La Rissole.

L'usage. Hé bien! soit. Je l'accepte.

Merlin.

Fatal, naval, régal, sont des mots qu'on excepte.
Pour peu qu'on ait de sens, ou d'érudition,
On sait que chaque règle a son exception.
Par conséquent on voit par cette raison seule——

La Rissole.

J'ai des démangeaisons de te casser la gueule.

Merlin.

Vous?

La Rissole.

Oui, palsandié! moi: je n'aime point du tout
Qu'on me berce d'un conte à dormir tout debout:
Lorsqu'on me veut railler, je donne sur la face.

Merlin.

Et tu crois au Mercure occuper une place,
Toi? Tu n'y seras point, je t'en donne ma foi.

La Rissole.

Mordié! je me bats l'œil du Mercure et de toi.
Pour vous faire dépit tant à toi qu'à ton maître,
Je déclare à tous deux que je n'y veux pas être:
Plus de mille soldats en auraient acheté
Pour voir en quel endroit La Rissole eût été:
C'était argent comptant; j'en avais leur parole.
Adieu, pays. C'est moi qu'on nomme La Rissole.
Ces bras te deviendront ou *fatals*, ou *fataux*.

Merlin.

Adieu, guerrier fameux par tes combats *navaux*.

this latter mode for the formation of the comparative. The Spanish and Portuguese languages retained *magis* (Sp. *mas*; Port. *mais*); but Italian and French exchanged it for the synonymous *plus* (Fr. *plus*, It. *più*). Neither *plurimum* nor *maxime*, however, were, on account of their unwieldly length, chosen for forming the superlative, the newly-formed definite article being selected for this purpose. Nevertheless a considerable number of comparatives in *or* and superlatives in *isme* occur in Old French : *granz, graignor, grandime ; mals, pejor, pire, pesme ; petit, meindre, minime* ; of *alt* is formed *altisme*; of *saint, saintisme ; ancien, ancienor,* and so on. The Modern French has preserved the Latin comparatives of *bon, petit, mauvais* in *meilleur, moindre, pire* ; and the Latin superlative in a number of words which are chiefly used in official language as titles of rank : *sérénissime, éminentissime, illustrissime, amplissime, réverendissime, nobilissime.* Frequently superlatives are formed with a tinge of irony according to this analogy: *richissime, savantissime, bellissime, savantissime, rarissime, vérissime, clarissime.* Besides this, a certain number of Latin comparatives and superlatives have been retained in Modern French, which, however, have lost their force as comparatives and superlatives : *citérieur, extérieur, inférieur, intérieur, majeur, mineur, postérieur, supérieur, ultérieur ; extrême, suprême, intime, prime, infime, minime.*

Of the Derivation of Adjectives.

§ 101. French adjectives are derived by means of suffixes from verbs, substantives, and other adjectives.

§ 102. A small number of Latin adjectives, derived from adverbs and prepositions, pass into the French language : *bénin* (bene, benignus), *quotidien* (quotidie, quotidianus), *antérieur* (ante, anterior), *postérieur* (post, posterior), *extérieur* (extra, exterior), *intérieur* (intra, interior), *supérieur* (supra, superior), *contraire* (contra, contrarius). French has but rarely formed any adjectives according to this analogy ; but we find : *moderne* (modo), *ancien* (ante), *souverain* (supra).

§ 103. The majority of the suffixes of adjectives are of Latin origin : *esque* and *asque* are received from the Italian; *ard* and *aud* from the German, and *et, ette* and *ot, otte* are of purely French formation. (See above, § 93.) The formative power of these suffixes varies greatly in degree. Latin suffixes, which are entirely effete, or nearly so, in French, are (*a*) for the formation of adjectives from verbs : *ax* (ace), *idus* (ide), *ilis* (ile), *icus* (ique), *icius* (ice), *bundus* (bond) ; and (*b*) for the formation of adjectives from substantives: *aceus* (acé), *alis* (al, el), *elis* (èle, el), *lentus* (lent), *e-stis, e-ster, -stris* (este, estre, être). More or less formative power is retained for forming adjectives from verbs by: *ivus* (if, ive), *bilis* (able, ible), *ard* (G. hart); and from substantives: *anus* (ain, en, an), *aneus* (ané), *inus* (in), *arius* (aire, ier, er), *t-orius* (t-oire), *osus* (eux), *atus* (é), *utus* (u); and from adjectives: *aster* (âtre), and (G. w-alt).

§ 104.   ADJECTIVES DERIVED FROM VERBS.

ax (ace): *efficace, fugace, rapace, tenace, vivace*. Sometimes substantives derived from this class of adjectives exist in French, though the adjective itself has not been received: *capacité, mordacité, véracité*.

idus (ide): *avide, cupide, intrépide, rapide, timide, lucide, rigide, valide*;—*cru* (crudus), *chaud* (calidus).

ilis (ile): *docile, ductile, fragile, utile, fertile, volatile, agile, habile, versatile, aquatile*;—*frêle* (fragilis), *grêle* (gracilis), *humble* (humilis).

icus (ique) is rarely preserved, since the final *c* is generally rejected (see § 27); as in *ami* (amicus), *fourmi* (formica), *ortie* (urtica), *vessie* (vesica); but we find *antique, pudique, classique, juridique, oblique*.

icius (ice): *factice, fictice*. More frequently preserved as a suffix of substantives in the form *is* (see § 65).

bundus (bond): *furibond, moribond, pudibond, vagabond*; —*fécond, rubicond*.

ivus (if, ive). Latin formations: *votif, actif, chétif, captif, fugitif, natif, naïf, négatif, purgatif, laudatif, furtif, vif*. French formations: *appréciatif, appréhensif, attentif, craintif, décisif, excessif, exploratif, expressif, évasif, fictif, hâtif, instructif, intuitif, plaintif, pensif, persuasif, vindicatif*. Derived from substantives: *oisif* (otium), *maladif* (maladie).

bilis (a-ble, i-ble). Latin formations: *aimable, terrible, dissoluble, voluble, capable, comparable, misérable*. French formations: *buvable, faisable, concevable, recevable, indéfinissable, saisissable, tarissable, tenable, soutenable, convenable, valable, redoutable, serviable, semblable, charitable, guéable, remarquable*. Many adjectives of French formation in *ible* prefer the Latin form of the verb to the French form: *indicible, disponible, exigible, corrigible, lisible, visible, flexible*. From a substantive is derived *paisible*.

ard (G. hart): *bavard, criard, mignard, nasillard, savoyard*. (See above, § 92.)

ADJECTIVES.

§ 105. ADJECTIVES DERIVED FROM SUBSTANTIVES.

eus (é): *éthéré, igné, silicé.*

aceus (acé): *herbacé, liliacé, papyracé, testacé, cétacé, farinacé.*

alis (al, el): *austral, boréal, capital, légal, loyal, pluvial, rural, vénal, virginal, naturel, officiel, spirituel, substantiel, ministériel, artificiel.* French formations: *essentiel, industriel, partiel, pestilentiel*; and from adjectives: *éternel, continuel, perpétuel, sempiternel.*

elis (èle, el): *fidèle, cruel.*

ilis (il, ile): *civil, gentil, puéril, subtil, viril, hostile, scurrile.*

lentus (lent): *opulent, pulvérulent, turbulent, violent, sanguinolent.*

ester, estris (este, estre, être): *agreste, céleste, équestre, pédestre, terrestre, champêtre.*

esque, asque. These suffixes have passed into the French language through the medium of the Italian. The Latins knew *iscus* as a suffix: *lentiscus, libyscus, mariscus, syriscus, cathaliscus, scutriscum.* But its use in Latin is so rare, that the influence of some other language only can explain the use made in Italian of *esco*. The Greeks have a diminutive suffix -ίσκος: ἀμφορίσκος, πινακίσκος, στεφανίσκος, παιδίσκη, μαζίσκη. But both in meaning and use the German suffix *isch* is most nearly related to the Italian *esco* and French *esque* and *asque*: *chevaleresque, grotesque, pittoresque, romanesque, tudesque, barbaresque, moresque, bergamasque, comasque, fantasque.*

anus (an, ain, en). Latin formations: *montouan, romain, humain, mondain, païen, vénitien, moyen (medianus).* Of French formation: *catalan, mahométan, persan, gallican, certain, hautain, lointain, prochain, souverain, vilain, républicain, ancien, alsacien. prussien, athénien, européen, italien, indien, phénicien, citronien, diluvien.*

aneus (ané, ain). Of Latin formation: *momentané, méditerrané, spontané.* Of French formation: *instantané, cutané, simultané.* The suffix *ain* has frequently arisen from a confounding of the two suffixes *anus* and *aneus*. From the Latin are: *forain* (foraneus, *from* foras), *soudain* (subitaneus), *souterrain* (subterraneus). From *extraneus* has been derived *étrange.*

inus (in). Of Latin formation: *latin, alpin, aquilin, canin, divin, léonin, libertin, marin, salin, voisin.* Of French formation: *badin, enfantin, mutin, gredin, sauvagin, poupin, angevin.*

From *galbinus* is derived *jaune*. *Oléagineux* is a new French formation of this class from *oleum*, with the suffix *eux* superadded.

arius (aire, ier, er). Words of original Latin formation mostly assume the form *aire*: *contraire, arbitraire, héréditaire, littéraire, sanguinaire, primaire, secondaire, quadragénaire, sexagénaire, adversaire, premier.* Words of French formation prefer the forms *ier* and *er*: *altier* (altus), *plénier* (plenus), *dernier* (de retro), *bocager* (bocage), *mensonger* (mensonge), *menager* (menage), *carnassier* (caro). Adjectives with this suffix are confounded with adjectives in *aris*: *populaire, pupillaire, salutaire, vulgaire, molaire, familier, régulier, séculier, singulier.*

t-orius (t-oire). This suffix is more generally used in French for the formation of substantives. Latin formations presuppose a nomen agentis in *tor*, but French adjectives may be formed by *toire* from verbal bases, without the intervention of a substantive in *tor*: *oratoire, méritoire, aratoire, transitoire, dinatoire, sécrétoire.*

osus (eux). This is one of the most fertile suffixes of the Romance languages for the formation of adjectives from substantives. Original Latin as well as Modern French formations are abundant: *aqueux* (aquosus), *belliqueux* (bellicosus), *envieux* (invidiosus), *épineux* (spinosus), *montueux* (montosus), *pierreux* (petrosus), *impérieux, ambitieux, noueux, glorieux, précieux.* Of French formation: *boiseux, paresseux, frileux, ombrageux, courageux, capricieux, soigneux, peureux, soucieux, haineux, dangereux, chanceux, ennuyeux, goutteux, hideux, bourbeux, douteux, laiteux, légumineux.* A few are derived from primary adjectives: *pieux* (pius), *doucereux* (dulcis), *sérieux* (serius). One only takes the form *oux*: *jaloux* (zelus, ζῆλος); and one the form *ose*: *morose* (morosus).

atus (é). A large number of French adjectives are formed after the analogy of the Latin participle perfect. In Latin, participles in *atus* (*é*) are the most numerous, and this form is therefore usually adopted by analogous derivatives in French. But those in *utus* (Fr. *u*) are likewise rather frequent. Of Latin formation are: *ailé* (alatus), *crêté* (cristatus), *étoilé* (stellatus). Of French formation are: *affairé, agé, ardoisé, denté, hérissonné, lézardé, maniéré, sensé, potelé, perlé, mouflé, naufragé, lacinié.*

utus (u). Some Latin forms in *atus* assume in French a form like those in *utus*: *barbu* (barbatus), *chevelu* (capillatus), *crépu* (crispatus), *cornu* (cornutus). Of French formation:

bossu, bourru, branchu, crochu, feuillu, grappu, herbu, grenu, joufflu, membru, moussu, pansu, poilu, pointu, fourchu, charnu, goulu, têtu, touffu, ventru.

§ 106. ADJECTIVES DERIVED FROM ADJECTIVES.

Many of the suffixes by which adjectives are derived from substantives are also used for deriving secondary adjectives from primary adjectives.

aster (âtre) is used in words of modern formation chiefly for modifying the meaning of adjectives expressing colour: *bleuâtre, grisâtre, blanchâtre, jaunâtre, olivâtre, brunâtre, roussâtre, verdâtre*; sometimes as a depreciative: *douceâtre, acariâtre, folâtre, opiniâtre, bellâtre, gentillâtre.*

et: *aigret, clairet, doucet, duret, follet, grasset, jeunet, paillet, joliet, longuet, mollet, brunet, seulet.* Frequently with the intercalation of another suffix: *aigrelet, grandelet, maigrelet, nettelet, rondelet.*

ot: *vieillot, bellot, ragot, manchot.*

aud (O. H. G. walt): *salaud, lourdaud, noiraud, sourdaud.* (Compare § 92.)

OF THE NUMERALS.

§ 107. The French cardinal numbers from one to sixteen follow the Latin. In *septendecim* (dix-sept) transposition takes place; the subtraction in *duodeviginti* and *undeviginti* is replaced by addition in *dix-huit, dix-neuf*; the decads from twenty to sixty follow again the Latin method; but from seventy to ninety they are expressed by addition and by scores. The manner of counting by scores was carried even farther in Old French: *treis vinz* (60), *treis vinz et dis* (70), *six vinz* (120), *sept vinz* (140), *huit vinz* (160), *onze vinz* (220), *quatorze vinz* (280). Some remnants of this habit of counting by scores are still to be found in Modern French; as, *les quinze-vingts*, an asylum for the blind in Paris, receiving three hundred inmates. One of these inmates is called *un quinze-vingt*. Vertot says: *Il s'était trouvé dans six vingts combats.* The manner of counting by scores is familiar to the Celtic languages, and to the Basque. The French cardinal numbers and their orthography were settled about the thirteenth century.

§ 108. The Old French formed distinct cases for the nominative and accusative of the first three cardinal numbers:

Nom.	uns, une	dui, doi	troi, trei
Acc.	un, une	dous, deus	troi, treis

§ 109. Collective substantives are formed from the cardinal numbers by the suffix *aine*: *une huitaine, une douzaine, une dizaine, une quinzaine, une vingtaine, une trentaine*. As metrical terms occur the masculine forms *quatrain, sixain, huitain, dizain*.

§ 110. The substantive *zéro* is derived from the Arabic *çifron*, a cypher.

§ 111. The ordinal numerals from three upwards are formed by the suffix *ième* (esimus). *Second* is being gradually displaced by the more modern formation *deuxième*. Already *deuxième* is used exclusively in the compound numerals (*vingt-deuxième, trente-deuxième*), where the Old French used also *second*. So likewise it has become obsolete to say *second* after the name of a sovereign, and *deux* is used instead.

§ 112. A few remnants of the Latin ordinal numerals are to be found in *Charles Quint, Sixte Quinte, la tierce partie, le quart denier, le tiers état, le tiers ordre de St. François, la fièvre tierce*. Even Lafontaine says: *un quart voleur survient*. *Primus* is found in the expressions *de prime abord, de prime saut*.

§ 113. The Latin distributive numerals are lost in French. They are replaced most frequently by the reduplication of the cardinal numbers: *un à un, deux à deux, trois à trois*, for *singuli, bini, terni*. Other means of replacing them are, e.g. 'Une multitude de chars attelés chacun de quatre chevaux' (Bernardin de St. Pierre). 'Ces tableaux valent cent francs chacun' (Bescherelle). 'Deux fois par semaine; de deux jours l'un' (Acad.). Some of the roots of the distributive numerals have been preserved in derivatives; e.g. *biner, binage, binaire, terne, quaterne, quinaire, senaire*.

§ 114. The multiplicative numeral has been preserved in French, although it is customary to avoid some; e.g. *milluple*. The Latins also avoided certain of these forms (*quadragesuplex*). In ordinary use are: *simple, double, triple, quadruple, quintuple, sextuple, septuple, octuple, nonuple, décuple, centuple, multiple*.

OF THE PRONOUNS.

As in Latin, so in the Romance tongues, more peculiarities of declension are found in the inflection of the personal than of the relative demonstrative or possessive pronouns. The latter resemble in their use and changes the more ordinary adjectives.

§ 115. Some Latin pronouns, as *hic, is, uter, ullus, alius*, have been lost in French. On the other hand, a variety of new

PRONOUNS.   83

pronouns are formed by the composition of pronouns with pronouns, or of pronouns with particles, which are so intimately fused as to make it sometimes difficult to recognise the component parts. No new pronouns are formed by derivation. Several substantives (*homo, res, persona*) and particles (*inde, ibi*) receive pronominal force and discharge the functions of pronouns, and even a Latin genitive (*illorum*) is raised to the dignity of a new independent pronoun.

§ 116. All French pronouns have a double form, the conjunctive and the disjunctive. The former, a monosyllable, stands before the verb or noun, and is in its nature a true proclitic, having no separate existence. On the other hand, the disjunctive pronoun has a fuller form and has a separate existence, resembling the noun in every respect. The personal pronouns have an enclitic form not only for the nominative and accusative, but also for the dative. Only the genitive is wanting, and is replaced by the adverb *inde* (en).

In Old French this distinction between conjunctive and disjunctive pronouns was not strictly observed. Its origin may perhaps be found in the Celtic, which uses the radical consonant of a pronoun as an enclitic or proclitic between other words. Irish: *m* instead of *me* (I), *te* for *tu* (thou), *n* for *ni* (we); in the oblique cases these forms are used almost exclusively.

PERSONAL PRONOUNS.

§ 117. In Old French the Personal Pronouns assume the following forms:—

Sing.	eo, jeo, jo, je	tu	—
	de mi, etc.	de ti	de si, etc.
	a mi, etc.	a ti	a si
	mi, moi, mei	ti, toi, tei	si, soi, sei
Plur.	nos, nous, nus	vos, vous, vus	—
	de nos, etc	de vos	de si
	a nos, etc.	a vos	a si
	nos, nous, nus	vos, vous, vus	si, soi, sei

Sing.	il	ele	
	de lui	de lei, de lui	
	a lui	a lei, a lui	
	lui	lei, lui	
Plur.	il (els)	eles	
	d'els	d'eles	
	a els	a eles	
	els	eles	

The oldest French form of the pronoun of the first person is *eo*. This *eo* becomes by *diphthongaison* (see § 29) *ieo, jeo,* and then both *jo* and *je*. The Burgundian dialect prefers *je* (ju), the Picardian *jou*, and the Norman *jeo, je*. In the oblique cases of the personal pronouns, the forms *mi, ti, si*, are Burgundian; *moi, toi, soi,* are Picard; and *mei, tei, sei,* belong to the Norman dialect. In the plural, *nos, nous* are Burgundian, *nus* Norman, whilst the Picard uses *no* for the nominative, and *nos* for the oblique cases. *Lui* was used exclusively for the masculine till the middle of the thirteenth century; the Burgundian had a feminine form *lei*. Instead of *ele*, many MSS. use the abbreviation *el*, pl. *els*. The Modern French form *ils* is found first in the beginning of the fourteenth century.

Out of these various dialectic forms Modern French retained two, the Burgundian and the Picard. The Burgundian forms (*me, te, se*, etc.) were set aside for the conjunctive pronoun; the Picardian forms (*moi, toi, soi*, etc.) were retained as exclusively disjunctive pronouns. This is a beautiful instance of the manner in which a written language recruits its resources from the spoken dialects.

In Old French the personal pronouns frequently formed contractions with relative pronouns, conjunctions, and adverbs: *jel* (je le), *mes* (me les), *tus* (tu les), *sis* (si les), *neu* (ne le), *nes* (ne les), *kil* (ke il), *quel* (que le), *quis* (qui les), *eissis* (eissi· les). These contractions are no longer permitted in Modern French.

The nominatives *je, tu, il,* and *ils*, are, through their constant association with the verb, losing their separate existence, and begin to be replaced by their accusatives, whenever the pronoun has the tonic accent; as, *c'est toi, est-ce lui*?

Possessive Pronouns.

§ 118. The Latin possessive pronouns are formed from the genitive of the personal pronouns; thus, *meus* from *mei*, *tuus* from *tui*, and so on. Besides the French possessive pronouns derived directly from the Latin pronouns, a new one has been formed according to the Latin analogy, *leur* from *illorum*.

The forms of the possessive pronouns were very numerous in the thirteenth century. To classify these numerous forms and clearly to explain their formation is rendered peculiarly difficult by the fact that many of these pronouns either are or appear defective. The dialects appear to have mingled at a comparatively early period, or to have borrowed from each other the forms in which they were respectively defective. Nevertheless, two complete and distinct groups of possessive pronouns have been developed in Modern French out of the Old French forms, one group being composed of conjunctive and the other of disjunctive pronouns.

The Burgundian singular and plural forms which are derived from Latin singular forms are shown in the subjoined tables:

		Masc.	Fem.
Sing.	*Nom.*	mes, tes, ses	ma, ta, sa
	Acc.	mon, ton, son	ma, ta, sa
Plur.	*Nom.*	mei, tei, sei	mes, tes, ses
	Acc.	mes, tes, ses	mes, tes, ses

These forms exhibit a close analogy to the Latin forms. The nominatives singular masculine (*mes, tes, ses*) are evidently the Latin *meus, tuus, suus*; whilst the accusatives singular masculine are the Latin accusatives *meum, tuum, suum*. The nominative plural and accusative plural are not less easily distinguished, whilst the feminine forms of the singular point to *mea, tua, sua*, and in the plural to *meas, tuas, suas*. For the formation of the Modern French pronouns, we have only to take the accusatives of the Burgundian pronoun, a process which is in analogy with other formations of the language.

But another group of pronouns are derived from the singular of the Latin pronouns by the suffix *en*:—

		Masc.	Fem.
Sing.	*Nom.*	miens, tuens, suens	meie, teie, seie
	Acc.	mien, tuen, suen	meie, teie, seie
Plur.	*Nom.*	mien, tuen, suen	meies, teies, seies
	Acc.	miens, tuens, suens	meies, teies, seies

These pronouns became afterwards, when used with the definite article, the modern disjunctive pronouns.

From the Latin plural pronouns are derived:—

		Masc. and Fem.		
Sing.	*Nom.*	noz	voz	lor
	Acc.	(no)	(vo)	lor
Plur.	*Nom.*	noz (no)	voz (vo)	lor
	Acc.	noz	voz	lor

These furnished the modern conjunctive pronouns, whilst the disjunctive were developed from the following:—

		Masc.	Fem.
Sing.	*Nom.*	nostres, vostres	nostre, vostre
	Acc.	nostre, vostre	nostre, vostre

	Masc.	Fem.
Plur. Nom.	nostre, vostre	nostres, vostres
Acc.	nostres, vostres	nostres, vostres

The two groups which furnished the disjunctive pronouns exhibit the Old French declension in its greatest strictness. Even now the disjunctive pronouns are used frequently as conjunctive pronouns, especially after an indefinite article: *un mien frère, une mienne cousine* (Acad.); *un mien cousin, un mien ami* (La Fontaine); *un mien pré* (Racine); *un mien valet, un sien portrait* (Voltaire).

Instead of *ma, ta, sa,* the modern language substitutes *mon, ton, son,* in order to avoid the hiatus. The old language preferred elision: *tame, symage, mesperance.* To this day *m'amie* is usual, but its etymology being forgotten, is spelled *ma mie.*

Demonstrative Pronouns.

§ 119. The French demonstrative pronouns are derived from the Latin *iste, ille* by composition with *ecce.* These compound pronouns had their origin in the popular language of Rome, and are of frequent occurrence in the comic poets, especially in Plautus: 'Set generum nostrum ire *eccillum* video cum adfini suo' (*Trin.* iii. 1, 21). 'Aput nos *eccillam* festinat cum sorore uxor tua' (*Stichus* iv. 1, 30). 'Tegillum *eccillut* mihi unum aret: id si vis dabo' (*Rudens* ii. 17, 18). 'Certe *eccistam* video' (*Curcul.* v. 2, 17). The Old French compounds of *ecce ille* and *ecce iste* are:—

		Masc.	Fem.
(a.)	Sing. Nom.	cist, cestui	ceste, cestei
	Acc.	cest, cestui	ceste, cestei
	Plur. Nom.	cist	cestes
	Acc.	cez	cestes

Or, without throwing off the initial *i*: *icestui*, etc.:—

		Masc.	Fem.
(b.)	Sing. Nom.	cil, celui	cele, celei
	Acc.	cel, celui	cele, celei
	Plur. Nom.	cil	celes
	Acc.	cels	celes

Or, without throwing off the initial *i*: *icelui, icele,* etc.

The indeclinable *ce* (O. F. *ceu, ceo*) is derived from *ecce hoc.*

The Norman dialect differed but little in the form of these pronouns from the Burgundian; the Picardian dialect of course changes the Burgundian *c* into *ch*: *chil, chele, chelui.*

After the thirteenth century these pronouns began to be

used in their present form and acceptation. The distinction between the conjunctive, derived from *iste*, and the disjunctive, derived from *ille*, was inherent in the meaning of their etymons. As long as their terminations distinctly showed their derivation from *iste* and *ille*, the enclitic *ci* and *là* were not used.

The forms with initial *i* are still in use in legal parlance: *Je vais exposer à vos yeux l'idée universelle de ma cause, et les faits renfermés en icelle* (Racine). *Trois procureurs, dont icelui Citron a déchiré la robe* (Id.). *Cettui* is still used by Lafontaine : *Cettui Richard était juge. Cettui me semble, à le voir, Papimane.*

§ 120. Relative and Interrogative Pronouns.

The relative and interrogative pronouns have been identical from the very oldest time. As interrogative sentences were formed in the modern language by construction, the use of special pronouns was no longer a necessity. The two pronouns used as interrogatives and relatives are *qui* and *quel* (qualis). *Quoi* is a secondary form of *qui*; its derivation from *quid* seems inadmissible, since it would imply a continued distinction between interrogatives and relatives, to which the whole evidence is opposed. *Dont* (de unde) was used originally in the sense of *d'où*, but gradually exchanged its adverbial force for that of a genitive of the relative pronoun. In the old language it was mostly replaced by *cui*. *Quel*, like other Latin adjectives of two terminations, had in Old French but one termination for the two genders, but began to have a separate form for the feminine in the first half of the thirteenth century. It was used at all times with or without the article.

§ 121. Indefinite Pronouns.

Some of the Latin indefinite pronouns have not been preserved in French : *quidam, nemo, omnis*. On the other hand new ones have been formed by the composition of pronouns with pronouns, and by employing substantives as pronouns.

From substantives are derived : rien (O. F. *riens*, acc. *rien*), rem ; on (O. F. *homs*), homo ; *personne*, persona.

The derivation of the following is plain enough : —

autre, *alter*	quiconque, *quicunque*
autrui, *alter*	quelconque, *qualiscunque*
chaque, *quisque*	tout, *totus*
chacun, *quisque unus*	nul, *nullus*
quelque, *qualisquam*	tel, *talis*
quelqu'un, *qualisque unus*	aucun, *aliqui unus*

Plusieurs is a comparative formed from a comparative, a form like *pluriores*. A similar aberration of grammar is found in the German *mehrere*.

Beaucoup, literally, a fine stroke. The derivation from *bella copia* is inadmissible; *copia* is in French, and never could be anything but *copie*. The *u* of *coup* is evidently a vocalised *l*. Compare the Italian *colpire*, to strike.

Même from *semet ipsissimus*, or rather from a contracted form like *met-ipsimus*.

Maint, from Goth. *manags*, O. H. G. *manac*, M. G. *manch*.

Some Old French indefinite pronouns have been lost in Modern French:—

    al, el (*aliud*)
    alquant, alkant, anquant (*aliquantus*)
    molt, mult; pl. mulz, multes (*multus*)
    nesun, nisun (*ne ipsum unus*)
    nuns (*ne unus*)
    nelui, nului (*nullus*)

OF THE VERB.

§ 122. French Verbs have been divided by descriptive grammarians into four regular conjugations, according to the termination of their infinitives. These four infinitives—*er, ir, oir* and *re*—they represent as corresponding to the Latin infinitives in *are, ire, ēre,* and *ĕre* respectively. According to the last edition of the Dictionnaire de l'Académie, more than 3,400 verbs end in the infinitive in *er*, 350 in *ir*, about 50 in *oir*, and about 240 in *re*. It will be seen presently that not all verbs in *oir* are derived from verbs in *ēre*, some being from verbs in *ĕre*, whilst those in *er*, though chiefly derived from verbs of the first Latin conjugation, are also derived from verbs of the three other conjugations. This passage of verbs from one conjugation into the other had begun in the classical period of the Latin tongue, as fervēre and fervĕre, frendēre and frendĕre testify.

§ 123. Comparative grammarians reduce the ordinary four Latin conjugations to two,—the Vowel Conjugation and the Consonant Conjugation. The latter contains those verbs whose crude form ends in a consonant or *u* (*v*), i.e. the third conjugation of ordinary grammars; the former those whose crude form ends in one of the vowels *ā, ē, ī*, i.e. the first, second, and fourth conjugations of ordinary grammars. The chief distinction of these conjugations is seen in the formation of the perfect, which is formed in the consonant conjugation (*a*) by appending the suffix *i* to the crude form, and lengthening the radical vowel if it should happen to be short: *lĕg-o, lēg-i*; *in-cūd-o, cud-i*; (*b*) by prefixing the reduplication: *posc-o, po-posc-i*; *pang-o, pe-pig-i*; (*c*) by the use of the connecting consonants *s* or *v*, which latter after a consonant is changed into *u*: *carp-o, carp-s-i*; *col-o, col-u-i*. The vowel conjugation forms its perfect by appending *vi* to the crude form: *amā-vi, delē-vi, audi-vi*.

Applying this principle to the French conjugation, we shall find that the three conjugations in *er, ir*, and *re* are the representatives of the Latin vowel conjugation; whilst that in *oir* continues the consonant conjugation.

§ 124. The first French conjugation (*er*) contains, besides a large number of Latin verbs in *are*—*aimer* (amare), *porter* (portare), *chanter* (cantare), *appeler* (appellare), *créer* (creare)—a great many of the consonant conjugation (in *ĕre*): *affluer* (affluĕre), *céder* (cedĕre), *contribuer* (contribuĕre), *ériger* (erigĕre), *négliger* (negligĕre), *opprimer* (opprimĕre), *obstruer* (obstruĕre), *resister* (resistĕre), *tisser* (texĕre); and a great many in *ēre*, which belong partly to the vowel and partly to the consonant conjugation: *absorber* (absorbēre), *exercer* (exercēre), *persuader* (persuadēre), *revérer* (reverēri). Verbs in *ire* rarely pass into the first French conjugation: *tousser* (tussire), *mouiller* (mollire), *chatouiller* (catulire), of which *mouiller*, *chatouiller* seem to presuppose some intermediate form like *molliare, catulliare*.

§ 125. The second French conjugation must be subdivided in two classes: (*a*) verbs of the simple or primitive form; and (*b*) verbs of the enlarged or inchoative form. From a desire of having a fuller and more expressive form, the French language frequently adopted the Latin inchoative form, simply on account of its fuller sound, and without assigning to it any other meaning than that of the Latin primitive. Or the Latin inchoative suffix gradually lost its force. The Latin inchoative form is confined to the French present (sing.) and imperfect (sing. and pl.), indicative and subjunctive (sing. and pl.), and to the participle present. Originally confined to verbs from the Latin in *esco*—*noircir* (nigrescere), *éclaircir* (exclarescere), *gémir* (in-gemiscere), *fleurir* (florescere), *durcir* (durescere), *rougir* (rubescere), *palir* (palescere), *abolir* (abolescere)— the French inchoative form was gradually extended to verbs, which have no corresponding etymon in *esco*: *périr, punir, finir, ravir, régir*. Besides Latin verbs in *īre*, the second French conjugation contains a large number of verbs in *ĕre* of the consonant conjugation, and in *ēre*, which partly follow the consonant conjugation : *agir* (agĕre), *applaudir* (applaudĕre), *convertir* (convertĕre), *fléchir* (flectĕre), *frémir* (fremĕre), *ravir* (rapĕre), *régir* (regĕre), *trahir* (tradĕre), *fuir* (fugĕre), *envahir* (invadĕre), *cueillir* (colligĕre), *fleurir* (florēre), *resplendir* (resplendēre), *abolir* (abolēre), *emplir, remplir, accomplir* (implēre). A few are derived from O. H. G. verbs in *jan* : *haïr* (hatjan), *rôtir* (rostjan), *fournir* (frumjan), *fourbir* (furbjan), *choisir* (chiusan), *honnir* (honjan), *brandir, bruir, croupir, garnir, meurtrir*.

§ 126. The French conjugation in re (commonly called the fourth) differs from the simple or primitive form of the second only by its infinitive in re and its past participle in u. It contains verbs in *ĕre* : *vendre* (vendĕre), *craindre* (tremĕre), *fendre* (findĕre); with several in *ēre* : *tondre* (tondēre), *semondre* (semonēre), *répondre* (respondēre), *mordre* (mordēre), *tordre* (torquēre).

§ 127. Though the French conjugation bears such a striking resemblance to the Latin conjugation, that their identity cannot for a moment be doubted, yet we see at a glance that a large number of the Latin inflections have been entirely lost, or are in a greatly advanced state of phonetic decay.

The deponent verbs, wherever they are preserved in French, have assumed the active form : *consoler* (consolari), *suivre* (sequi), *naître* (nasci), *mourir* (mori), *imiter* (imitari). This process of changing the active form for the deponent had made considerable progress amongst the verbs of the first conjugation, even in the classical period. Cicero and Virgil use both *populo* and *populor*, *munero* and *muneror*. Cicero prefers the forms *auspicor, oscitor, fabricor*, whilst Plautus and Terence, together with the later writers, say *auspico, oscito, fabrico*. Also deponent verbs of other conjugations began to assume the active form, like *partiri* and *dispertiri*. A gradual transition seems observable in the infinitive *moriri* : *Cupidus moriri* (Ov. *Metam.* xiv. 215). *Moriri sese misere mavolet, quam non perfectum reddat quod promiserit* (Plaut. *Asin.* i. 1, 108). *Set nunc se ut ferunt res fortunæque nostræ, moririst par nec meliust morte in miseriis* (Id. *Rud.* iii. 3, 12). But in Low Latin all deponents are conjugated like the active voice.

The passive voice was defective even in Latin, and the wanting tenses and moods were expressed by periphrasis with the verb *esse*. This method was extended in French to the remaining tenses and moods. Only the perfect participle of the passive (*amatus, aimé*) was retained, as its existence was necessitated by the periphrastic formation of the passive. The infinitive also, which in Latin was only distinguished by the final *e* or *i*, retains its passive force, and the French infinitive, after rejecting the distinguishing mark, may be considered as a fusion of the Latin infinitive active and passive: *Cette marchandise est à prendre, à laisser. Cela est à faire, à revoir, à recommencer* (Acad.). *Une seule remarque reste à faire* (Châteaubriand).

The loss of the Latin passive voice and the deponent is replaced in French by the reflective or pronominal verb: *Le spectacle se donnait* (dabatur) *en l'honneur des dieux* (Mme. de Staël). *Rien ne s'y voyait plus* (videbatur), *pas même des débris* (De Vigny). *Un cri s'entend* (auditur) (Alfred de Vigny). This use of the reflective verb, instead of the passive, seems quite natural, when we consider the intimate connexion between the two forms. The Latins had many passive forms with a purely reflective meaning: *delector, crucior, fallor, feror, commoveor, inclinor, mutor, vertor*.

§ 128. The gradual phonetic decay of the Latin conjugation, the connexion of the Modern French conjugation with it and its derivation, will be best seen by comparing the subjoined simple tenses of the Old French regular conjugation, in the Burgundian dialect, with the corresponding Latin and Modern French tenses.

INDICATIVE.

Present.

I.	II. *a.*	II. *b.*	III.
chant(e)	part	flor-is (x)	vend
chant-es	par-s (z)	flor-is	ven-s (z)
chant-et	part-et, part	flor-ist	vend-et, vend
chant-ons	part-ons	flor-issons	vend-ons
chant-eiz, -ez	part-eiz	flor-isseiz	vend-eiz
chant-ent	part-ent	flor-issent	vend-ent

Imperfect.

chant-eve	part-oie	flor-issoie	vend-oie
chant-eves	part-oies	flor-issoies	vend-oies
chant-evet	part-oit	flor-issoit	vend-oit
chant-iens	part-iens	flor-issiens	vend-iens
chant-iez	part-iez	flor-issiez	vend-iez
chant-event	part-oient	flor-issoient	vend-oient

Perfect.

chant-ai	part-i	flor-i	vend-i
chant-as	part-is	flor-is	vend-is
chant-at	part-it	flor-it	vend-it
chant-ames	part-imes	flor-imes	vend-imes
chant-astes	part-istes	flor-istes	vend-istes
chant-arent	part-irent	flor-irent	vend-irent

Future.

I.	II. a.	II. b.	III.
chant-erai	part-irai	flor-irai	vend-rai
chant-eras	part-iras	flor-iras	vend-ras
chant-erat	part-irat	flor-irat	vend-rat
chant-erons	part-irons	flor-irons	vend-rons
chant-ereiz	part-ireiz	flor-ireiz	vend-reiz
chant-eront	part-iront	flor-iront	vend-ront

CONJUNCTIVE.

Present.

chant-e	part-e	flor-isse	vend-e
chant-es	part-es	flor-isses	vend-es
chant-et	part-et	flor-isset	vend-et
chant-iens	part-iens	flor-issiens	vend-iens
chant-iez	part-iez	flor-issiez	vend-iez
chant-ent	part-ent	flor-issent	vend-ent

Imperfect.

chant-asse	part-isse	flor-isse	vend-isse
chant-asses	part-isses	flor-isses	vend-isses
chant-ast	part-ist	flor-ist	vend-ist
chant-assiens	part-issiens	flor-issiens	vend-issiens
chant-assiez	part-issiez	flor-issiez	vend-issiez
chant-assent	part-issent	flor-issent	vend-issent

CONDITIONAL.

chant-eroie	part-iroie	flor-iroie	vend-roie
chant-eroies	part-iroies	flor-iroies	vend-roies
chant-eroit	part-iroit	flor-iroit	vend-roit
chant-eriens	part-iriens	flor-iriens	vend-riens
chant-eriez	part-iriez	flor-iriez	vend-riez
chant-eroient	part-iroient	flor-iroient	vend-roient

IMPERATIVE.

chant-e	part	flor-is	vend
chant-eiz	part-eiz	flor-isseiz	vend-eiz

INFINITIVE.

chant-eir, -er	part-ir	flor-ir	vend-re

GERUND.

chant-ant	part-ant	flor-issant	vend-ant

PARTICIPLE.

chant-eit, -eie	part-it, -ie	flor-it, -ie	vend-uit, -uie

CONJUGATIONS.

§ 129. From this it appears that the only inflected Latin tenses preserved in French are the indicatives of the present, imperfect and perfect, the conjunctives of the present and plusquamperfectum, the imperative and infinite active, and of the passive voice only the participle perfect. The subjoined tables show the Latin suffixes with their corresponding Old French and Modern French representatives. The dialectic variations are given in the column of Old French suffixes.

I. FIRST CONJUGATION.

INDICATIVE.

Present.

Latin.	Old French.				Modern French.	
-ŏ					-e	
-ās	-es				-es	
-ăt	-et	-ed	-e		-e	
-āmŭs	-ons	-omes	-ommes	-um	-ons	
-ātĭs	-eiz	-es	-ez		-ez	
-ant	-ent				-ent	

Imperfect.

-ābăm	-eve	-oie	-oue		-ois	-ais
-ābăs	-eves	-oies	-oues		-ois	-ais
-ābăt	-evet	-oit	-out		-oit	-ait
-ābāmŭs	-iens	-iemes	-iomes	-ium	-ions	
-ābātĭs	-ieiz	-ies	-iez		-iez	
-ābant	-event	-oient	-ouent		-oient	-aient

Perfect.

-āvī	-ai				-ai
-āvistī	-ais	-as			-as
-āvĭt	-ait	-at	-ad	-a	-a
-āvĭmŭs	-ames	-asmes			-âmes
-āvistĭs	-astes				-âtes
-āvērunt -ēre	-erent (-arent)				-èrent

CONJUNCTIVE.

Present.

-ĕm	-e				-e	
-ēs	-es				-es	
-ĕt	-et	-ed	-e		-e	
-ēmŭs	-iens	-ions	-iemes	-iom	-ium	-ions
-ētĭs	-ieiz	-ies	-iez		-iez	
-ent	-ent				-ent	

Plusquamperfect.

Latin.	Old French.				Modern French.
-avissĕm	-aisse	-asse			-as
-avissēs	-aisses	-asses			-asses
-avissĕt	-aist	-ast			-ât
-avissēmus	-assiens	-assions	-assiemes	-assium	-assions
-avissētĭs	-assieiz	-assies	-assiez		-assiez
-avissent	-aissent	-assent			-assent

Imperative.

-ā	-(e)	-e

Infinitive.

-ārĕ	-eir (-ier) -er	-er

Gerund and Participle.

-andum -antem -atus	}	-ant -eit -et -ed -e	-ant -é

§ 130. II. SECOND CONJUGATION.

(a.) Simple Form.

Indicative.

Present.

-ĭo					-s	
-īs	-z	-s			-s	
-ĭt	-t				-t	
-īmŭs	-ons	-omes	-ommes	-um	-ons	
-ītĭs	-eiz	-es	-ez		-ez	
-iunt	-eut				-ent	

Imperfect.

-iēbăm	-oie	-eie			-ois	-ais
-iēbăs	-oies	-eies			-ois	-ais
-iēbăt	-oit	-eit			-oit	-ait
-iēbāmŭs	-iens	-iemes	-iomes	-ium	-ions	
-iēbātĭs	-ieiz	-ies	-iez		-iez	
-iēbant	-oient	-eient			-oient	-aient

Perfect.

-īvī	-i			-is	
-īvietī	-is			-is	
-īvĭt	-it	-i		-it	
-īvĭmŭs	-imes	(-ismes)		-îmes	
-īvistĭs	-istes			-îtes	
-īvērunt, -ērĕ	-irent			-irent	

CONJUGATIONS.

CONJUNCTIVE.
Present.

Latin.	Old French.	Modern French.
-iăm	-e	-e
-iās	-es	-es
-iăt	-et -ed -e	-e
-iāmŭs	-iens -ions -iemes -iomes -ium	-ions
-iātĭs	-ieiz -ies -iez	-iez
-iant	-ent	-ent

Plusquamperfect.

-ivissĕm	-isse	-isse
-ivissēs	-iesses	-isses
-ivissĕt	-ist	-ît
-ivissēmŭs	-issiens -ssions -assiemes -assium	-issions
-ivissētĭs	-issieiz -issies -issiez	-issiez
-ivissent	-issent	-issent

IMPERATIVE.

-ī	—	-e

INFINITIVE.

-īre	-ir	-ir

GERUND AND PARTICIPLES.

-iendum }	-ant	-ant
-ientem }		
-itus	-it -i	-i

§ 131.   (b). *Enlarged or Inchoative Form.*

INDICATIVE.
Present.

-isco -esco	-is	-is
-īs	-is	-is
-ĭt	-ist	-it
-īmŭs	-issons, etc.	-issons
-ītĭs	-issieiz, etc.	-issez
-iunt	-issent	-issent

Imperfect.

-escēbăm	-issoie, etc.	-issois	-issais
-escēbās	-issoies, etc.	-issois	-isssis
-escēbăt	-issoit, et c	-issoit	-issait
-escēbāmŭs	-issiens, etc.	-issions	
-escēbātĭs	-issieiz, etc.	-issiez	
-escēbant	-issoient	-issoient	-issient

Perfect.
(As in the Simple Form.)

Conjunctive.
Present.

Latin.	Old French.	Modern French.
-escăm	-isse	-isse
-escās	-isses	-isses
-escăt	-isset, etc.	-isse
-escāmŭs	-issiens, etc.	-issions
-escātĭs	-issieiz, etc.	-issiez
-escant	-issent	-issent

Plusquamperfect.
(As in the Simple Form.)

Gerund and Participle.

| -escendum
-entem } | -issant | -issant |

§ 132. III. *THIRD CONJUGATION.*
Indicative.
Present.

-eŏ	—	-s
-ēs	-z -s	-s
-ĕt	-t	-t
-ēmŭs	-ons, etc.	-ons
-ētĭs	-eiz, etc.	-ez
-ent	-ent	-ent

Imperfect.

-ēbăm	-oie	-eie	-ois	-ais
-ēbās	-oies	-eie	-ois	-ais
-ēbăt	-oit	-eit	-oit	-ait
-ēbāmŭs	-iens, etc.		-ions	
-ēbātĭs	-ieiz, etc.		-iez	
-ēbant	-oient	-eient	-oient	-aient

Perfect.

-ēvī	-i		-is
-ēvistī	-is		-is
-ēvĭt	-it	-i	-it
-ēvĭmŭs	-imes (-ismes)		-îmes
-ēvistĭs	-istes		-îtes
-ēvērunt	-ērĕ	-irent	-irent

Conjunctive.
Present.

-eăm	-e	-e
-eās	-es	-es
-eăt	-et, etc.	-e
-eāmŭs	-iens, etc.	-ions
-eātĭs	-ieiz, etc.	-iez
-eant	-ent	-ent

CONJUGATIONS.

Imperfect.

Latin.	Old French.	Modern French.
-evissem	-isse	-isse
-evisses	-isses	-isses
-evisset	-ist	-ît
-evissēmŭs	-issiens, etc.	-issions
-evissētĭs	-issieiz, etc.	-issiez
-evissent	-issent	-issent

IMPERATIVE.

| -ō | — | -s |

INFINITIVE.

| -ēre | -re (-oir) | -re (-oir) |

GERUND AND PARTICIPLE.

| -endum
 -entem } | -ant | -ant |
| -etus(-uitus, -utus) | -uit -ut -ud -u | -u |

No account is taken in the above table of verbs whose preterite ends in *us, us, ut, ûmes, ûtes, urent*, which are small in number, and follow the consonant or irregular conjugation. In the regular verb, the following forms (using the customary French names) are identical: (*a.*) the indicative imperfect and subjunctive present, with the exception of the enlarged second conjugation; (*b.*) the preterite, with the exception of the first conjugation; (*c.*) the participle present, with the exception of the enlarged form of the second conjugation.

§ 133. A new tense and a new mood are formed in French by using the abbreviated present and imperfect of the auxiliary verb *avoir* (habere) as suffixes; viz. the future and conditional: *aimer-ai, aimer-as, aimer-a* = *amare habeo, habes, habet* and *aimer-ais* (*avais*), *aimerais* (*avais*), *aimerait* (*avait*) = *amare habebam, habebas, habebat.*

§ 134. A comparison of the above tables shows the following general results as to the personal suffixes of verbs:—

(*a.*) Unaccented vowels of personal suffixes, whether final or not, are rejected: *sens* (sentio and senti), *sentes* (sentias), *pars* (partio and parti), *aimons* (amamus). In Modern French the rejection of a final vowel is sometimes marked by a mute *e*, where in Old French simply the stem of the verb was used: M. F. *chante*, O. F. *chant*, L. *canto*; M. F. *aime*, O. F. *aim*, L. *amo*; M. F. *supplie*, O. F. *supply*, L. *supplico*.

(*b.*) Final consonants, especially *m* and *t*, are rejected:

F

aime (amem, amat, amet), *dormisse* (dormivissem), *mentant* (mentiendum, mentientem), *aimas*, (amasti), *fini*, (finitus).

(*c.*) Syncope of a vowel and consonant takes place in the second person plural, where of *tis* only the final *s* or *z* remains: *aimez* (amatis), *êtes* (estis), *partites* (partivistis).

(*d.*) An inorganic *s*, which makes its first appearance in the fourteenth century, is gradually added to the first person of the present of the second and third conjugation (*finis, pars, vends*; but not in *j'ouvre, je souffre*, etc.), and to the first person of all imperfects (*aimais, finissais, vendais*). This *s* had probably its origin in a confusion of the first and second persons. In some instances, as in imperatives before *y* and *en*, its origin is euphonic: *vas-y, cueilles-y, donnes-en*. In forms ending in a double vowel this *s* was not used by Molière, Corneille, and Racine, who wrote: *je croi, voi, sui, je tien*, etc. Poets have retained these forms in rhymes to the present day:—

Eh ! vous n'êtes donc pas sorcier?—Pas plus que toi.
Mais que savez-vous donc?—Je sais ce que je voi.

Ponsard.

(*e.*) The *t* of the third person singular, which was preserved in Old French, has been lost in the affirmative and negative form of the verb in Modern French. In the interrogative form it is still preserved both in writing (between two hyphens) and in pronunciation: *a-t-il, aime-t-il, aima-t-il, aimera-t-il*.

(*f.*) The forms *ois* and *ais* belonged originally to different dialects, but gradually the latter form became general. In 1675 Bérain, avocat au parlement de Rouen, proposed the substitution of *ais* for *ois*. Latouche, in his 'Art de bien parler Français' (1694), teaches that *chantois, chanterois*, etc., are to be pronounced *chantais, chanterais*. The form *ais* became universal through its adoption by Voltaire, and is hence commonly called the Voltairian orthography. The change was sanctioned by the Académie only in 1835. The change was further extended to verbs in *oître* and their derivatives—*connaître, connaissance*; instead of *connoître, connoissance*; to some other verbs, as *faiblir* instead of *foiblir*; and to adjectives in *ois*: *Anglais, Français*, instead of *Anglois, François*. To the present day we find *harnois, roide, roidir, roideur*, as well as *harnais, raide, raidir, raideur*, though the latter seems to be the more usual form in speaking. The old form and pronunciation have been preserved in *Hongrois, Vaudois, Chinois, Génois, Carthaginois*, etc.

(*g.*) The final *r* of the infinitive was audible in Old French. The Picardian form *ier* was gradually displaced by the Norman form *er*. In the process of rejecting the dialectic *i*, Modern French has occasionally rejected an *i* belonging to the stem, as in *commencer* (com-initiare), *embrasser* (im-bracchiare).

(*h.*) All verbs of the simple form of the second conjugation end, with the exception of *fuir*, in their crude forms in a double consonant: *ment-ir*, *dorm-ir*, *serv-ir*. They therefore throw out the final *n*, *m*, *t* or *v* of the crude form before *s* and *t*, in order to prevent the accumulation of three consonants: *dors, dort*; *mens, ment*; *repens, repent*; *sens, sent*; *pars, part*; *sors, sort*; *sers, sert*. *Vêtir*, having rejected *s* before *t*, forms its present according to the general rule, i.e. *vêts*, like *fuis* from *fuire*.

(*i.*) Verbs of the second conjugation, whose crude form ends in *ll, vr, fr*, take, instead of the inorganic *s*, an *e*: *saille, cueille, ouvre, couvre, offre, souffre*, and take throughout the indicative and subjunctive present the inflections of the first conjugation. Only *bouillir* takes *s*: *je bous*.

In the future *cueillir*, with its compounds *accueillir, recueillir* follows the first conjugation: *cueillerai*, etc.

(*k.*) Verbs of the third conjugation differ from the simple form of the second only by their infinitive in *re* and the past participle in *u*. In the third person singular of the present indicative, verbs of this conjugation, whose crude form ends in *d*, retain this *d* and reject the inflectional *t*: *il répond*, instead of *répond-t*. In *battre*, one *t* is rejected before an inflectional *t* or *s*: *je bats, il bat*. In *coudre*, which stands for *cousr'e* (consuere), the original Latin *s* reappears in *cousons, cousis, cousu* (consutus).

(*l.*) Verbs with an intercalated *d* (*ndre*), from the Latin verbs in *ngere, nguere* and *mere*, throw out the intercalated *d* of their infinitives and futures in the monosyllabic forms of the present and imperative. In all other forms of more than one syllable, they change *n* in *ng*. To this class belong: *ceindre* (cingere), *éteindre* (extinguere), *étreindre* (stringere), *contraindre* (constringere), *astreindre, restreindre* (restringere), *feindre* (fingere), *enfreindre* (infringere), *peindre* (pingere), *plaindre* (plangere), *teindre* (tingere), *atteindre* (attingere), *joindre* (jungere), *conjoindre, déjoindre, disjoindre, enjoindre, oindre* (ungere), *poindre* (pungere), *épreindre* (exprimere), *empreindre* (imprimere). *craindre* (tremere, O. F. cremer, cremir, crembre).

IV. CONSONANT CONJUGATION.

§ 135. The consonant conjugation is older than the vowel or regular conjugation. The tendency of the language is to absorb verbs of the consonant conjugation gradually into the vowel conjugation, whence it happens that many verbs belonging in Latin to the former have been received in French into the latter, particularly those in *indre* and *uire*.

§ 136. As in Latin the perfect is made the criterion for distinguishing the conjugation of a verb (see § 123), so in French the corresponding tense, the preterite, is the form according to which verbs are classified in the consonant conjugation. Their infinitives, which are the guides of descriptive grammarians, end either in *oir*, *re*, or *ir*. They are divided into the following three classes:—

(*a.*) Verbs which form their preterite by modifying the radical vowel into *i* and without adding any temporal suffix: inf. *ven-ir*, pret. O. F. *ving*, *vinc*. The final *s* of the Modern French *vins* is inorganic. (See § 134 *d*.)

(*b.*) Verbs which form their preterites in an *s*, which has its origin in an *s* of the Latin consonant conjugation: *mis* (misi), *conclus* (conclusi), *dis* (dixi), *fis* (feci; compare faxim, faxo).

(*c.*) Verbs which form their preterite in *us* (O. F. *ui*). The Old French termination *i* was rejected when the inorganic *s* was added to the first person. The termination *us* shows itself especially in the preterite of verbs in *oir*, which are derived from Latin verbs in *ēre* with a perfect in *ui*: M. F. *dus*, O. F. *dui*, L. *debui* (debēre); M. F. *tus*, O. F. *tui*, L. *tacui* (tacēre); M. F. *voulus*, O. F. *voului*, L. *volui* (volēre). But it has been subsequently extended to other verbs, especially those which form their Latin perfects in *vi*, *bi*, *pi*: M. F. *connus*, O. F. *conui*, L. *cognovi* (cognoscĕre); M. F. *crûs*, O. F. *crui*, L. *crevi* (crescĕre); *mus* (movi), *repus* (pavi), *résolus* (resolvi); M. F. *bus*, O. F. *bui*, L. *bibi* (bibĕre); M. F. *conçus*, O. F. *concui*, L. *concepi* (concipĕre), *reçus* (recēpi, recipĕre).

§ 137. The following tables show the conjugation of the three forms of the preterite of the consonant conjugation both in Old and Modern French:—

(a.) *First Class.*

INDICATIVE.

Old French.	Modern French.
vi	vis
veis	vis
vit	vit
veimes (ismes)	vîmes
veietes	vîtes
virent	virent

SUBJUNCTIVE.

veisse	visse
veisses	visses
veist, etc.	vît, etc.

(b.) *Second Class.*

INDICATIVE.

dis	dis
desis, deis	dis
dist	die
desimes, deimes, dismes	dîmes
desistes, deistes	dîtes
distrent, dissent, disent, dirent	dirent

SUBJUNCTIVE.

desisse, deisse	disse
desieses, deisses	disses
desist, etc.	dît

(c.) *Third Class.*

INDICATIVE.

dui	dus
deus	dus
dut	dut
deumes, dusmes	dûmes
deustes	dûtes
durent	durent

SUBJUNCTIVE.

deusse	dusse
deusses	dusses
deust, etc.	dût, etc.

The termination of the past participle of the consonant conjugation is, like that of the preterite, threefold: (*a*) *u* (O. F.

uit, ut), which generally represents the Latin *itus*: *dû* (debitus), *connu* (cognitus); (*b.*) *s*, which chiefly represents Latin participles in *sus*: *mis* (missus), *pris* (prensus, prehensus); (*c*) *t*, from Latin participles in *tus*: *cuit* (coctus), *fait* (factus), *dit* (dictus). The first and third subdivision of these verbs form their past participle mostly in *u*, the second in *s* and *t*.

The following list contains all the Latin verbs of the consonant conjugation, which have been preserved in Modern French * :—

§ 138.   I. First Class.

Latin Inf.	French Inf.	Pret.	Past Part.
tenere	tenir	tin(s)	tenu
venire	venir	vin(s)	venu
videre	voir	vi(s)	vu

§ 139.   II. Second Class.

cædere	circon-cire	circoncis	circoncis
claudere	clore	clos	clos
dicere	dire	dis	dit
facere	faire	fis	fait
mittere	mettre	mis	mis
prehendere	prendre	pris	pris
ridere	rire	ris	ris
surgere	sourdre	—	—
trahere	traire	—	trait
quærere	con-quérir	conquis	conquis
sedere	as-seoir	assis	assis

§ 140.   III. Third Class.

habere	avoir	eus	eu
concipere	concevoir	conçus	conçu
calere	chaloir	(chalut)	(chalu)
cadere	dé-choir	dé-chus	dé-chu
debere	devoir	dus	dû
fallere	falloir	fallut	fallu
movere	mouvoir	mus	mu
pluere	pleuvoir	plut	plu
posse (=potere)	pouvoir	pus	pu
sapere	savoir	sus	su
valere	valoir	value	valu
velle (=volere)	vouloir	voulus	voulu

* Compound verbs are not included in this list; but where the simple verb has been lost in French, a representative compound has been chosen.

Latin Inf.	French Inf	Pret.	Past Part.
currere	courir	courus	couru
jacere	gésir	(jui, juc)	(jeut, jut)
mori (moriri)	mourir	mourus	mort
bibere	boire	bus	bu
credere	croire	crus	cru
crescere	croître	crûs	crû
legere	lire	lus	lu
molere	moudre	moulue	moulu
cognoscere	connaître	connus	connu
pascere	paître	re-pue	re-pu
parere(parescere)	paraître	parus	paru
placere	plaire	plus	plu
solvere	ab-soudre	ab-solus	ab-sous
tacere	taire	tus	tu
vivere	vivre	vēcus	vécu

§ 141. All the verbs in *oir* form their future like the verbs in *re*: *recevoir, recevrai*; *savoir, saurai* (savrai). Forms like *verrai, décherrai, pourrai* seem to indicate that assimilation has taken place in the infinitive *voir*=*verre*, *pouvoir*=*pourre*.

§ 142. The subjunctive of the present of these verbs retains, generally speaking, a greater resemblance to the Latin subjunctive than in verbs of the vowel conjugation: *sache* (sapiat), *vaille* (valeam), *voie* (videam), *sois* (sim).

§ 143. The first, second, and third persons singular, and the third person plural present of these verbs, shows a phenomenon which somewhat resembles the German modification of the radical vowel, although this resemblance is merely apparent, and has a very different origin. In *tiens, tient, tiennent*; *viens, vient, viennent*, and so on, this reinforcing of the vowel seems to have its origin simply in the desire to strengthen the monosyllabic form of the verb, inasmuch as the original vowel reappears as soon as a syllable is added to the word: *tenons, tenez*; *venons, venez*. In Old French this process was extended to many verbs of the vowel conjugation, as *aimer* and *donner*. The present of *aimer*, for instance, was:—

aim
aimmes, aimes
aimmet, aimme, aime
amons
ameiz, amez
aiment, aimment

§ 144. It has been attempted to divide all French verbs into two conjugations, the strong and the weak, on the basis of this modification or reinforcement of the radical vowel. The process, however, has a mere outward resemblance to the modification of the vowel in the German conjugation. In the latter, new tenses are formed by the modification of the vowel, whilst in French it serves simply to give a little more body to a fading form.

AUXILIARY VERBS.

§ 145. The lost tenses and moods of the active and the whole of the passive voice are expressed periphrastically by the participle perfect and the auxiliary verbs *avoir* and *être*. In the earlier stages of development the auxiliary *avoir* was also used with infinitives for the formation of tenses, and became gradually a new suffix for the formation of the future and conditional: *aur-ai* = *aver-ai* = *habere habeo*; *ser-ai* = *essere-habeo*; *aur-ais* = *habere habebam*; *ser-ai* = *essere habebam*.

§ 146. The verb *esse* had been used already by the Romans for the formation of several tenses and moods of the passive voice. Its extended use in French was a natural consequence of the loss of the inflected passive. The infinitive *être* was derived by Schlegel and Raynouard from *stare*. The use of *stare* for the formation of the imperfect, and the presence of the *t* support this view. On the other hand, the long *é* does not agree with this derivation. Diez and Burguy, therefore, derive *être* from *esse*, or rather from *essere*, like *tistre* (for *tis're*) from *texere*.* The Latin imperfect was preserved in the Old French: *ere, ieres, iert, erium, eriez, ierent*. But in the earliest records we find *stabam* used as the imperfect of this auxiliary verb. *Stare* is used even in classical Latin in some combinations where it closely approaches the use of an auxiliary verb: *Hannibal, postquam ipsi sententia stetit pergere ire* (Liv. xxi. 30). *Stat pectore fixum Æetæ sociare manus* (Val. Flacc. v. 289). And in the frequent phrase *per me stat*. Besides the imperfect *étais* (stabam), the past participle *été* (status), and the participle present *étant* (standum, stantem), are derived from *stare*.

§ 147. The verb *habere* was frequently used by the Latins with a participle perfect passive as a pregnant circumlocution for the perfect: *Inclusum in curia senatum habuerunt* (Cic. Att. vi. 2, 8). *Romulus habuit plebem in clientelas principum de-*

---

* Compare also *connaître* (cognoscere), *naître* (nascere).

scriptam (Id. *Rep.* ii. 9). *Si nondum eum satis habes cognitum* (Id. *Fam.* xiii. 17, 3). *De Cæsare satis dictum habebo* (Id. *Phil.* v. 19, 52).

§ 148. The following tables contain the simple tenses of the verbs *avoir* and *être* in the three dialects of the langue d'Oïl. The gradual phonetic decay will be apparent on comparing these forms with the corresponding Latin and Modern French forms :—

HABERE.

Burgundian.	Picardian.	Norman.
avoir	avoir (aveir)	aver

Habeo.

ai	ai	ai
as, ais	as	as
at, ait	at, a	ad
avons	avomes	avum
aveiz	aves	avez
ont	ont	unt

Habebam.

avoie	avoie	aveie
avoies	avoies	aveies
avoit	avoit	aveit
aviens	aviemes	avium
avieiz	avies	avies
avoient	avoient	aveient

Habui.

aüi, oi, o	éui, euc	u, ou
aüis, ois, os	éuis	us
aüit, oit, ot	éuit	ut
aümes, etc.	éuimes	umes
aüistes, etc.	éuistes	utes
aüierent, etc.	éuirent	urent

Habere habeo.

(aver-) aurai	aurai	aurai
aurais	auras	auras
aurait	aurat	aurad
aurons	aurommes	aurum
aureiz	aures	aurez
auront	auront	aurunt

Habere habebam.

aver- (aur-) oie	aver- (aur-) oie	aver- (aur-) eie
auroies	auroies	aureies
auroit	auroit	aureit
auriens	auriemes	aurium
aurieiz	auries	auriez
auroient	auroient	aureient

Habeat, etc.

Burgundian.	Picardian.	Norman.
aie	aie	eie
aiiens	aiemes	eium
aieiz	aies	eiez

Habeam.

aie	aie	eie
aies	aies	eies
ait	ait	eit
aiiens	aiemes	eium
aieiz	aies	eiez
aient	aient	eient

Habuissem.

aüsse	éuisse, éusse	usse
aüsses	éuisses	usses
aüst	éuist	ust
aüssiens	éuissiemes	ussum
aüssieiz	éuissies	ussiez
aüssent	éuissent	ussent

Habentem, habendum.

aiant	aiant	eiant

Habitus, a, um.

aüt	éut	ud

---

§ 149. **Esse (Essere).**

estre	iestre	estre

Standum, stantem.

estant	estant	estant

Status, a, um.

esteit	estet	ested

Sum.

suye, sui	sui	sui
es	ies	es
est	est	est
somes	sommes	sum
estes	iestes	estes
sont	sont	sunt

Stabam.

estoie	estoie	esteie
estoies	estoie	esteies
estoit	estoit	esteit
estiens	estiemes	estium
estiez	esties	estiez
estoient	estoient	esteient

AUXILIARY VERBS. 107

Fui.

Burgundian.	Picardian.	Norman.
fui	fui	fui
fuis	fus	fus
fuit	fut	fud
fuimes	fumes	fum
fuistes	fustes	fustes
furent	furent	furent

Esse(re) habeo.

serai	serai	serrai
serais	seras	serras
serait	serat	serrad
serons	seromes	serrum
sereiz	seres	serrez
seront	seront	serront

Esse(re) habebam.

seroie	seroie	serreie
seroies	seroies	serreies
seroit	seroit	serreit
seriens	seriemes	serrium
serieiz	series	serriez
seroient	seroient	serraient

Sis, etc.

sois	sois	seie
soiens	soiemes	seium
soieiz	soies	seiez

Sim.

soie	soie	seie
soies	soies	seies
soit	soit	seit
soiens	soismes	seium
soieiz	soies	seiez
soient	soient	seient

Fuissem.

fuise	fuisse	fusse
fuises	fuisses	fusses
fuist	fuist	fust
fuisiens	fuissiemes	fussum
fuisiez	fuissies	fussez
fuisent	fuissent	fussent

DERIVATION OF VERBS.

§ 150. Verbs are derived either from nouns or from primitive verbs. All derivative verbs follow the vowel conjugation; the majority the first in *er*, and a few the second in *ir*. A modification of the vowel of the base is of rare occurrence: *digne, daigner*; *bas, baisser*;—*droit, dresser*; *faim, affamer*. The final consonant of the base frequently undergoes phonetic changes, the principal of which are: (*a*) Final *f* of the base changes into *v*; *chef, achever*; *sauf, sauver*. (*b*.) Final *x* changes into *s* or *ss*; *prix, priser*; *paix, apaiser*; *toux, tousser*. (*c*.) The final consonant is doubled: *tas, entasser*; *épais, épaisser*; *pas, passer*; *mol, mollir*. (*d*.) Latin consonants which have been rejected by the French base, reappear in the derivative: *corner* (cor, cornu). (*e*.) Nasal *n* changes into *gn*: *dédain, dédaigner*; *soin, soigner*; *gain, gagner*; also here the original forms *dignor*, etc., reappear, for from *main* is formed *manier*. (*f*.) A euphonic *t* is frequently added to bases ending in a vowel: *abri, abriter*; *clou, clouter*.

§ 151. I. Verbs may be derived from nouns in three distinct ways: (*a*) by adding the verbal suffix *er* to the nominal base; (*b*) by adding *er* to a derivative substantive or adjective; (*c*) by proper verbal suffixes.

(*a*.) From primitive substantives are derived: *ambrer*, (ambre), *ancrer* (ancre), *auner* (aune), *couper* (coup), *camper* (campus), *écumer* (écume), *fêter* (fête), *ganter* (gant), *gommer* (gomme), *larder* (lard), *monter* (mont), *venter* (vent). Those from adjectives end frequently in *ir*: *aigrir* (aigre), *blanchir* (blanc), *bleuir* (bleu), *blêmir* (blême), *chérir* (cher), *froidir* (froid), *maigrir* (maigre), *pâlir* (pâle). A few are derived from particles: *devancer* (devant), *joûter* (juxta), *outrer* (outre, ultra).

(*b*.) The restrictions observed by the Latins in forming verbs from nouns are broken down in the Lower Latinity, where we find such derivatives as *viaticare, medicinare, christianare, mirabiliare, occasionare, contrariare, consuetudinare, solatiare, vagabundare, parlamentare, sententiare*. In fact, nearly all derivative substantives gave rise to verbs. Occasionally the derivative verb prefers the vowel of the original noun, though derived from a French derivative: *contrarier, contraire, contrarius*. The following list contains verbs derived from almost all derivative nouns:—

ade (ata): barricader, pallisader, gambader.

age (aticum): avantager, ménager, ravager, outrager, voyager, envisager, partager, fourrager.

al (alis, ale): égaler, signaler.

ance, ence (entia): fiancer, sentencier, engeancer, différencier, licencier.

DERIVATION OF VERBS.

ard (hart): bavarder, mignarder, bombarder, nasarder.
as, asse, ace (aceus, acea): embarrasser, cuirasser, crevasser, grimacer.
âtre (aster): folâtrer, opiniâtrer.
ail, eil, il, ouil (a- e- i- u-culus, a, um): grailler, griller, aiguiller, grenouiller, verrouiller, gargouiller.
aim (amen): essaimer.
aire (arius): contrarier, salarier, vicarier.
aud (walt): badauder, courtauder, nigauder.
eau, el, elle (ellus, illus): agneler, bateler, bourreler, créneler, marteler, oiseler, amonceler.
èle, elle (ēla): quereller.
ent, ant (ens, ans, ntis): absenter, diligenter, présenter, patienter, serpenter, épouvanter, plaisanter, ensanglanter, enfanter.
esse, ice (itia): caresser, apparesser, justicier.
ice (itium): supplicier.
et, ette; ot, otte: breveter, cacheter, caqueter, feuilleter, loqueter, louveter, aiguilleter, chicoter, ballotter, mailleter, démailloter.
eul, ol (ŏlus): flageoler, rossignoler.
eur, our (or, ōris): savourer, labourer.
eux, oux (osus): jalouser, ventouser, creuser (corrosus).
ide (idus): liquider, intimider.
ier (arius): aciérer.
if (ivus): activer, joliver.
in, ine (inus): cheminer, discipliner, mariner, ruiner, enraciner.
on (o, ōnis): bouchonner, cramponner, crayonner, frissonner, gasconner, grisonner, rayonner.
on, ion, tion, son, çon (tio, sio): actionner, additionner, affectionner, cautionner, emprisonner, empoisonner, occasionner, raisonner, façonner, mentionner.
u (utus): bossuer.
us (utis): s'évertuer.
ule, cule, le (ulus, culus): formuler, craticuler, sangler.
ume (udinem): accoutumer.
ure (ura): aventurer, peinturer, manufacturer.
bond (bundus): vagabonder.
lent (lentus): violenter.
ment (mentum): alimenter, cimenter, parlementer, tourmenter, expérimenter.
time (timus): légitimer.

(*c.*) The suffixes which are used in Modern French for the

formation of verbs are mostly of Latin origin. The following are the principal suffixes:—

icare appears in French in the form of *iquer, cher, ger, guer* and *ier*. Words formed with this suffix in French generally prefer the latter form. Of Latin formation are: *fabriquer* (fabricare), *communiquer* (communicare), *revendiquer* (vindicare), *empêcher* (impedicare), *mâcher* (masticare), *prêcher* (predicare), *forger* (fabricare), *juger* (judicare), *manger* (manducare), *venger* (vindicare), *publier* (publicare), *communier* (communicare), *plier* (plicare). Of French formation are: *côtoyer* (côte), *fêtoyer* (fête), *flamboyer* (flambe), *foudroyer* (foudre), *coudoyer* (coude), *guerroyer* (guerre), *larmoyer* (larme), *ondoyer* (onde), *rudoyer* (rude), *nettoyer* (net). The forms *ayer* and *eyer* are varieties of this suffix: *bégayer* (bègue), *grasseyer* (parler gras).

issare, izare, is used as an equivalent of the Greek ἰζειν in *græcissare, atticissare* (ἑλληνίζειν, μηδίζειν). Originally it expressed imitation, but in Low Latin many verbs were formed by this suffix which express simply activity: *baptizare, scandalizare*. In French this suffix is very prolific: *centraliser, diviniser, fertiliser, latiniser, naturaliser, légaliser, fraterniser, autoriser, tranquilliser, brutaliser, maîtriser, économiser, pulvériser, ridiculiser, familiariser*.

escere (iscere), used originally for the formation of inchoative and intransitive verbs, gradually becomes a suffix for the formation of transitive and factitive verbs. Of Latin formation are: *durcir* (durescere), *éclaircir* (clarescere), *noircir* (nigrescere). French formations are: *étrécir* (étroit), *obscurcir, enforcir, accourcir, brunir, enchérir, affaiblir, enorgueillir, attendrir, vieillir*.

ulare (uler) is mostly used for forming verbs with a diminutive meaning. Of Latin formation are: *cumuler* (cumulare), *moduler* (modulari), *pulluler* (pullulare). Of French formation: *ebranler* (branca), *fourmiller* (formica), *habiller* (= habitulare).

ilare (iler): *ventiler* (ventilare), *bosseler* (bosse), *botteler* (botte), *chanceler* (chance), *harceler* (herse), *écarteler* (quart), *ensorceler* (sors).

aculare, iculare, uculare (ailler, iller, ouiller) are mostly used for the formation of frequentative and diminutive verbs: *égosiller* (gosier), *grappiller* (grappe), *boursiller* (bourse), *barbouiller* (barba, barbula), *rimailler, tirailler, mordiller, sautiller, gazouiller*.

eter and *oter* are used as diminutive and frequentative

suffixes: *buvoter, chevroter, clignoter, frisotter, gobelotter, vivoter, trembloter, feuilleter, marqueter, béqueter, chucheter, chuchoter.*

§ 152. II. Many Latin suffixes used for the formation of derivative verbs from primitive verbs, have been lost in French, and of those preserved, some have been productive of but few new derivatives.

tare (ter, ser). Of Latin formation are: *chanter* (cantare), *dicter* (dictare), *intenter* (intentare), *jeter* (jactare), *noter* (notare), *traiter* (tractare), *penser* (pensare), *pousser* (pulsare). Of French formation: *exécuter* (exsecutus), *exempter* (exemptus), *infecter* (infectus), *inventer* (inventus), *persécuter* (persecutus), *sculpter* (sculptus), *inciser* (incisus), *infuser* (infusus), *oser* (ausus), *professer* (professus), *raser* (rasus), *user* (usus), *fixer* (fixus), *oublier* (oblitus), *admoneter* (admonitus.)

itare (iter, eter). Of Latin formation are: *agiter* (agitare), *hésiter* (hæsitare), *palpiter* (palpitare). Of French formation: *graviter* (gravare). Both in Latin and French this suffix is sometimes used for the formation of verbs from nouns: *débiliter* (debilitare), *péricliter* (periclitari), *féliciter* (felix), *faciliter* (facilis), *habiliter* (habilis), *vanter* (vanus).

icare (cher, oyer) is very rarely used: *pencher* (=pendicare), *soudoyer* (= solidicare).

ulare (uler, ler). Of Latin formation: *ambler* (ambulare), *postuler* (postulare). Of French formation: *mêler, trembler, troubler.*

illare (iller, eler). Latin are: *titiller* (titillare), *vaciller* (vacillare). French formations: *gratteler, greneler.*

onner and *asser* are two verbal suffixes, the former formed from the Latin nominal suffix *o, ōnis*, the latter from the adjective suffix *aceus*, which are chiefly used for the formation of depreciatives: *chantonner, griffonner, nasillonner, rêvasser, écrivasser.*

OF THE ADVERB.

§ 153. French adverbs are either simple adverbs without any special adverbial suffix, or adverbs formed from adjectives by a suffix. Amongst the former class we must reckon adjectives formed by composition.

(*a.*) Simple adverbs: *où* (ubi), *y* (ibi), *là* (illac), *hier* (heri), *quand* (quando), *loin* (longe), *bien* (bene), *certes* (certe), *tard* (tarde), *mal* (male), *volontiers* (voluntarie).

Many adjectives are used as simple adverbs; but this use is mostly confined to certain phrases: *sentir bon, vendre cher, parler net, coûter cher, payer double, entendre dur, tenir ferme, jurer faux, peindre gras, voir juste, répondre sec, gagner gros, faire gras,* and many others.

(*b.*) Adverbs formed by composition were not uncommon in Latin : *extemplo, imprimis, invicem, obviam, posthac, adhuc, antehac, quapropter,* and so on. Only a few of these Latin formations have been preserved in French : *ailleurs* (aliorsum), *souvent* (subinde). But a number of new adverbs have been formed by the same process : *encore* (hanc horam*), *alors* (ad illam horam), *enfin* (in fine), *partout* (per totum), *depuis* (de post), *derrière* (de retro), *désormais* (de ipsa hora magis), *dorénavant* (de hora in ab ante), *ensemble* (in simul), *ici* (ecce hic), *jadis* (jam diu), *ça* (ecce hac), *dedans* (de[-d-]intus), *avant* (ab ante), *dehors* (de foras), *devant* (de ab ante), *dessus* (de susum), *dessous* (de subtus), *or* (hora), *demain* (de mane), *parfois* (per vices), *aussi* (aliud sic), *autant* (aliud tantum), *assez* (ad satis), *aval* (ad vallem), *amont* (ad montem).

This process of composition is continued with words of purely French form : *maintenant, aujourd'hui, auparavant, alentour, quelquefois, cependant,* and so on.

(*c.*) Adverbs are formed from adjectives by appending the suffix *ment.* This suffix has its origin in the feminine substantive *mens,* and consequently is appended to the feminine form of the adjective. The choice of *mens* as an adverbial suffix was peculiarly happy. Its ablative *mente,* joined to an adjective, serves even in Latin the purposes of an adverb : *Bona mente factum, ideoque palam ; mala ideoque ex insidiis* (Quinct. *Inst.* v. 10). *Quale sit id quod amas, celeri circumspice mente* (Ovid. *Rem. Am.* 89). *Ultro quin etiam devota mente tuentur* (Claud.). The oldest Italian manuscripts write *mente* as a separate word, and up to the sixteenth century it was customary to use *mente* only with the last of several adjectives : *Lo cavaliere fece la domanda sua umile e dolcemente* (*Nov. Ant.* 3). *Il padre loro rispose villana ed aspramente* (*Nov.* 19). Besides, *mens* is the unmistakeable representative of the Indo-European root *man,* which has been so extensively used both for composition and derivation. It occurs in *vehemens, vehementer ; demens, dementer ; amens, amenter ; mentio, mon-eo, mend-ax, me·min-i, Miner-va, commen-tum, comment-arius,* and all other derivatives in *mentum* and *mentarius.* It is found in Greek Μέν-τωρ, Ἀγα-μέμνων, μνήμη, μιμνήσκω, μῆνις, μνάομαι, μένος, μάντις. The many Latin substantives

---

* In Old French also *uncore* (unquam hora).

in *mentum* must have made the suffix familiar to the Latin ear. Latin authors of the tenth and eleventh century are fond of using *mente* with adjectives: *Fixa mente statutum habes, æqua mente, devota mente, tacita mente.* (For authorities, see Grimm, *Gram.* iv. 923.)

§ 154. In one instance a modern adverb is formed by the suffix *ment* from an original adverb: *comment* from *comme* (quomodo). The Old French had several such adverbs: *alsiment, ensement, ensemblement.*

Other attempts to form adverbs were not successful. Some remnants there are of adverbs in *ons*: *à reculons, à tâtons, à chevauchons.*

OF THE PREPOSITIONS.

§ 155. French prepositions are either original Latin prepositions, or compounds of prepositions with adverbs, adjectives or pronouns, participles, or substantives.

Latin prepositions are: *contre* (contra), *en* (in), *entre* (inter), *outre* (ultra), *par* (per), *pour* (pro), *sans* (sine), *sur* (super), *vers* (versus), *jouxte* (juxta).

By composition of Latin prepositions are formed: *avant* (ab ante), *depuis* (de post), *devant* (de ab ante), *devers* (de versus), *envers* (in versus).

By composition of prepositions with adverbs, adjectives and pronouns are formed: *dans* (de intus), *deçà* (de ecce hac), *delà* (de illac), *derrière* (de retro), *dessous* (de subtus), *dessus* (de sursum, susum), *après, d'après* (ad pressum), *parmi* (per medium), *selon* (secundum longum), *à travers* (ad transversum), *aveo* (apud hoc), *dès* (de ipso).

Participles used as prepositions are: *durant, joignant, moyennant, nonobstant, pendant, suivant.*

Prepositions derived from substantives are: *chez* (casa), *faute* (It. falta, faltare), *manque* (mancus), *malgré* (malum gratum).

Latin adjectives and adverbs used as French prepositions: *près* (pressum), *proche* (propius), *hors* (foras), *hormis* (foras missum).

OF CONJUNCTIONS.

§ 156. Many Latin conjunctions have been lost in French, others have been preserved with a changed meaning. New conjunctions have been formed by composition.

From the Latin have been preserved: *et* (et), *ni* (neque), *ou* (aut), *quand* (quando), *comme* (quomodo), *si* (si), *que* (quod, quam). With a different meaning have been preserved: *mais* (magis, *for* potius, autem, *and* sed), *car* (quare *with the meaning of* nam), *donc* (tunc *instead of* igitur), *tandis que* (tam diu quam *instead of* dum), *quoique* (quidquam *instead of* quamquam), *piusque* (postquam *instead of* quoniam).

By composition are formed, amongst others: *néanmoins* (nec ens minus *for* nihilominus), *aussi* (aliud sic *instead of* etiam, quoque), *encore* (hanc horam), *lorsque, alors que* (ad illam horam quod), *sans que* (sine quod), *après que* (ad pressum quod), *parce que* (per ecce istud quod), and a large number of compound conjunctions, whose origin and meaning require no further explanation.

OF COMPOUND WORDS.

§ 157. A large number of the compound words of the French language have been received as compounds from the Latin; others have been formed according to analogy. Some of the old compounds have been so welded together, that at the present day they present the aspect of simple words. A considerable number of the compounds of modern formation are mere *parasyntheta*, or words syntactically dependent on each other and connected in writing and speaking so as to form one word, such as: *bon-heur, casse-noisette, arc-en-ciel, fainéant, li-cou*. Of importance for the organic development of the language is only the composition with particles.

§ 158. Composition of substantives with substantives: *lundi* (lunæ dies), *mardi* (Martis dies), *mercredi* (Mercurii dies), *jeudi* (Jovis dies), *vendredi* (Veneris dies), *samedi* (sabbati dies), *connétable* (comes stabuli), *merluche* (maris lucius), *champart* (campi pars), *autruche* (avis struthio), *oripeau* (auri pellem), *orfèvre* (auri faber), *oriflamme* (auri flamma), *salpêtre* (sal petræ), *héberge* (G. heri-berga), *haubert* (G. hals-perc), *loup-garou* (L. lupus; G. werwolf), *Montmartre* (mons martyrum), *Finistère* (finis terræ), *Abbeville* (abbatis villa), *Chatelleraut* (castellum Eraldi).

§ 159. Composition of substantives with adjectives: *banqueroute* (banca rupta), *outarde* (avis tarda), *vinaigre* (vinum acre), *romarin* (ros-marinus), *dimanche* (dies dominica), *raifort* (radix fortis), *Vaucluse* (vallis clausa). Compounds of modern formation are generally connected by a hyphen: *aigue-marine* (alga marina), *pont-levis, taille-douce, main-forte, eau-forte, fer-blanc, cerf-volant, pot-pourri.*

§ 160. The adjectives precede the substantives in: *aubépine* (alba spina), *printemps* (primum tempus), *bonheur* (bonum augurium), *malheur* (malum augurium), *midi* (media dies), *minuit* (media nocte), *primevère* (prima veris), *Courbevoie* (curva via), *Clermont* (clarus mons), *Chaumont* (calvus mons). Modern compounds with the hyphen: *basse-cour, chauve-souris, franc-maçon, beau-père, belle-mère, grand-père, petit-fils, sauf-conduit,* and many others.

§ 161. The composition of verbs with substantives and adjectives is almost confined to imitations of the Latin compounds with *facere* (ficare). Direct from the Latin are: *édifier, modifier, signifier, purifier, multiplier, amplifier,* and many others. Imitated are, with substantives: *moinifier, ossifier, pétrifier, vitrifier, ramifier, personnifier.* With adjectives: *dulcifier, acidifier, rectifier, vérifier, qualifier, identifier.* Very large is the number of apparent compounds formed by the imperative of the verb and the accusative of a noun: *casse-cou, garde-fou, passe-temps, porte-faix, porte-manteau, tire-bouchon, tire-bottes, trouble-fête, coupe-gorge, essuie-main, chauffe-pieds, rendez-vous.* And graphically connected: *vaurien, fainéant.*

§ 162. Two adjectives are frequently united by a hyphen into one: *vert-blanc, clair-obscur, premier-né.* Formations like *anglo-français,* which were some short time ago greatly objected to, have nevertheless obtained currency. Littré uses *novo-latin* instead of Raynouard's hybrid form *néo-latin.*

§ 163.   *Composition with Particles.*

All the Latin prepositions are used in Modern French for forming compounds. Even those which have lost their existence as separate words (*cum, ex, præ*) are used as prefixes. The Greek prepositions are used only in words derived directly from the Greek. ἀντί, however, has entered the popular language: *anti-constitutional, anti-social,* etc.

§ 164. Decomposita, or words with two prefixes, are of more frequent occurrence in French than in Latin, owing to the large number of compounds which were received ready-made from Latin, and which to the Frenchman appear simple words: *re-dé-faire, as-su-jettir.* A triple prefix occurs in *re-com-en-c-er* (re-cum-in-iti-are).

With respect to assimilation, French prefixes follow the same phonetic laws as Latin prefixes.

A great difficulty is the use of the graphic accents over the prefixes *de* and *re*. *De* seems to be always accented, excepting (*a*) before a double sibilant (*ss, sc*) and before *st*. (*b*) In the adverbs *debout, deçà, delà, dehors, demain, demi, depuis, derechef, derrière, devant* and its derivatives *devancier, devanture*. (*c*) In *demander, demeurer, deviser, deviner*, and their derivatives. In *degré* the prefix is not accented in writing; but according to the best authorities, in speaking. *Demoiselle* is not a compound with *de*, but from *dominus* (compare *damoiseau*). As to the accentuation of the prefix *re*, no principle whatever seems to have been followed. It is, however, always accented before a vowel: *réédifier, réitérer*. *Pré* is always accented, excepting before *ss, sc* and *st*: *pressentir, prescrire, prestance*.*

§ 165. The following qualitative and quantitative adverbs are likewise used as prefixes: *bien* (bene), *mal* (male), *més, mé* (minus), *bis, bi* (bis), *demi* (dimidium), and the negative particles *in* (im, il, ir) and *non*.

* The present system of French accentuation is scarcely a hundred years old, and of very slow growth. The Neufchatel Bible of 1535 has not a single accent, which is the more striking as in its orthography (*faict, soubs,* for *fait, sous,* etc.) the influence of grammatical theories is evident. The acute accent on the final *é* seems to have been the first written accent used. Towards the end of the sixteenth century the grave accent is used as a mark of distinction over *à, où,* etc. The use of the circumflex over *ê* instead of *es* (*même* instead of *mesme*) is severely censured by the Academy in the preface to the first edition of its Dictionary. Jacques Dubois (sixteenth century) was the first who had a regular, though somewhat whimsical, system of accentuation. Up to the end of the last century considerable diversity prevailed as to accentuation. In an edition of Crébillon (2 vols. 4to. Imprimerie Royale, 1750), every word appears accented as at present, with the additional use of the circumflex over *vû, pû, aperçû,* and so on. The Geneva edition of Rousseau, in thirty volumes, of 1782, and a Paris edition of Montesquieu, of 1782, have, as far as I have observed, the system now in use. Bayle and the Dictionnaire de Trévoux use accents with great carelessness in the commonest words. The grave accent on the penultimate is regularly discarded in an edition of Racine of as late a date as 1799 (Paris: P. Didot l'aîné). Who was the inventor of the present system? Not the Academy, which simply followed the received usage. Nor Voltaire, who was notoriously careless as to spelling, but who, if he had invented it, would at least have laid down a guiding principle. Beza used accents; but I have no means of consulting his book. The plan of Du Guez (An Introductorie for to learn French trewly: London, no date, probably published about 1550) of writing accents below the line, is evidently a mere device for the use of foreigners.

APPENDIX.

SPECIMENS OF OLD FRENCH.

9TH CENTURY.

LES SERMENTS DE STRASBOURG.

Ergo XVI kalend. marcii Lodhuwicus et Karolus in civitate, quæ olim Argentaria vocabatur, nunc autem Strâzburg *vulgo dicitur, convenerunt, et sacramenta, quæ subter notata sunt, Lodhuwicus romana, Karolus vero teudisca lingua juraverunt. Ac sic ante sacramentum circumfusam plebem alter teudisca, alter romana lingua alloquuti sunt. Lodhuwicus autem, qui major natu, prior exorsus sic cœpit: ' Quotiens Lodharius me et hunc fratrem meum,' etc. Cumque Karolus hæc eadem verba romana lingua perorasset, Lodhuvicus, quoniam major natu erat, prior hæc deinde se servaturum testatus est:*

Pro deo amur et pro christian poblo et nostro commun salvament, d'ist di en avant, in quant deus savir et podir me dunat, si salvarai eo cist meon fradre Karlo et in adjudha et in cadhuua cosa, si cum om per dreit son fradra salvar dist, in o quid il mi altresi fazet, et ab Ludher nul plaid numquam prindrai, qui meon vol cist meon fradre Karle in damno sit.

Sacramentum autem, quod utrorumque populus quique propria lingua testatus est, romana lingua sic se habet: Si Lodhuvigs sagrament, que son fradre Karlo jurat, conservat, et Karlus meos sendra de sua part non los tanit, si io returnar non l'int pois, ne io ne neuls cui eo returnar int pois, in nulla ajudha, contra Lodhuvig nun li iv er.

CANTILÈNE DE SAINTE EULALIE.

Buona pulcella fut Eulalia,
bel avret corps, bellezour anima.
voldrent la veintre li deo inimi,
voldrent la faire diaule servir.
elle non eskoltet les mals conselliers,
qu'elle deo raneiet, chi maent sus en ciel,
ne por or ned argent ne paramenz,
por manatce, regiel ne preiement.
niule cose non la pouret omqi pleier,
la polle sempre non amast lo deo menestier.

e poro fut presentede Maximiien,
chi rex eret a cels dis sovre pagiens.
il li enortet, dont li nonqi chielt,
qued elle fuiet lo nom christiien.
ell' ent adunet lo suon element,
melz sostendreiet les empedementz,
qu'elle perdesse sa virginitet:
poros furet morte a grand honestet.
enz enl fou la getterent, com arde tost.
elle colpes non avret, poro nos coist.
aezo nos voldret concreidre li rex pagiens;
ad une spede li roveret tolir lo chieef.
la domnizelle celle kose non contredist,
volt lo seule lazsier, si ruovet Krist.
in figure de colomb volat a ciel.
tuit oram, que por nos degnet preier,
qued auuisset de nos Christus mercit
post la mort et a lui nos laist venir
par souue clementia.

10TH CENTURY.

LA PASSION DU CHRIST.

Christus Jhesus den s'enleved,
Gehsesmani vil' es n'anez.
toz sos fidels seder trovet
e van orar; sols en anet.
Granz fu li dols, fort marrimenz.
si condormirent tuit ades.
Jhesus cum veg, los esveled,
trestoz orar ben los manded.
Et dunc orar cum el anned,
si fort sudor dunques suded,
que cum lo sangs a terra curren
de sa sudor las sanctas gutas.
Als sos fidels cum repadred,
tam beulement los conforted.
li fel judeus ja s'aproiemed
ab gran cumpannie dels judeus.
Jhesus cum vidrit los judeus,
zo lor demande que querent.
il li respondent tuit adun
' Jhesum querem Nazarenum.'
' Eu soi aquel,' zo dis Jesus.
tuit li felun caden ginols.
terze ves lor o demanded,
a totas treis chedent envers.
Mais li felun tuit trassudad
vers nostre don son aproismad.
Judas li fel ensenna fei
' celui prendet cui baisarai.'

APPENDIX.

Judas cum veggnet ad Jhesum,
semper li tend lo sou menton;
Jhesus li bons nol refuded,
ad tradetur baisair doned.
   'Amicx,' zo dis lo bons Jhesus,
'per quem trades in ço baizol?
melz ti fura non fusses naz
que me tradas per cobetad.'
   Armad esterent evirum,
de totas part presdrent Jhesum;
nos defended ne nos usted,
a la mort vai cum uns anel.

11TH CENTURY.

LA CHANSON DE ROLAND.

CHANT IV.

Morz est Rollans : Deus en ad l'anme es cels!

Li emperere en Renceval parvient;
Il nen i ad ne veie, ne senter,
De voide tere nen alne ne plein pied
Que il n'i ait o Franceis o paien.
Carles escriet: 'U estes vos, bels nies?
U est l'arcevesque e li quens Oliver?
U est Gerins e sis cumpainz Gerers?
U est [dux] Otes e li quens Berengers?
Ive e Ivorie, que jo aveie tant cher?
Que est devenuz li gascuinz Engeler,
Sansun li dux e Anseis li hers?
U est Gerard de Russillun li veilz?
Li .xii. per que jo aveie laiset?'
De ço qui calt, quant nul n'en respundiet?
'Deus, dist li reis, tant me pois esmaer
Que jo ne fui al estur cumencer!'
Tiret sa barbe cum home ki est iret;
Plurent des oilz si baron chevaler,
Encuntre tere se pasment .xx. millers,
Naimes li dux en ad mult grant pitet!

Il nen i ad chevaler ne barun
Que de pitet mult durement ne plurt;
Plurent lur filz, lur freres, lur nevolz
E lur amis e lur lige seignurs;
Encuntre tere se pasment li plusur!
Naimes li dux d'iço [i] ad fait que proz,
Tuz premereins 'l ad dit l'empereur
'Veez avant de dous liwes de nus:
Veder puez les granz chemins puldrus,
Que asez i ad de la gent paisnur!
Car chevalchez, vengez ceste dulor!'

—'E Deus, dist Carles, ja sunt il ja si luinz!...
Cunseilez mei e [le] dreit et [l']honur;
De France dulce m'unt tolute la flur!'
Li reis cumandet Gebuin e Otun,
Tedbalt de Reins e le cunte Milun :
'Guardez le champ e les vals e les munz,
Lessez gesir les morz tut cum il sunt :
Que n'i adeist ne beste ne lion,
Ne n'i adeist esquier ne garçun ;
Jo vus defend que n'i adeist nuls hom
Josque Deus voeile que en cest camp revengum.'
E cil respundent dulcement par amur :
'Dreiz empereres, cher sire, si ferum.'
Mil chevaler i retiennent des lur. Aoi.

 Li empereres fait ses graisles suner,
Puis si chevalchet od sa grant ost li ber.
De cels d'Espaigne, [ki] unt lur les dos turnez,
Tenent l'enchalz : tuit en sunt cumunel.
 Quant veit li reis le vespres decliner,
Sur l'erbe verte descent [il] en un pred ;
Culchet sei a tere, si priet damne Deu
Que le soleil pur lui face arester,
La nuit targer e le jur demurer.
Ez vuz un angle ki od lui soelt parler,
Isnelement si li ad commandet :
'Charles, chevalche, car tei ne falt clartet !
La flur de France as perdut, ço set Deus ;
Venger te poez de la gent criminel !'
A icel mot l'emperere est muntet. Aoi.

 Pur Karlemagne fist Deus vertuz mult granz
Car li soleilz est remés en estant!
Paien s'enfuient, ben les enchalcent Franc ;
El Val Tenebres, la, les vunt ateignant ;
Vers Sarraguce les enchalcent li Franc,
A colps pleners les en vunt ociant,
Tolent lur veies e les chemins plus granz ;
L'ewe de Sebre el lur est de devant,
Mult est parfunde, merveilluse e curant ;
Il n'i ad barge ne drodmund ne caland ;
Paiens recleiment un lur deu Tervagant,
Puis saillent enz ; mais il n'i unt guarant ;
Li adubez en sunt li plus pesant ;
Envers les funz s'en turnerent alquanz,
Li altre en vunt [en] cuntreval flotant.
Li miez guariz en unt boüd itant,
Tuz sunt neiez par merveillus ahan ;
Franceis escrient : 'Mar veistes Rollant !' Aoi.

 Quant Carles veit que tuit sunt mort paien,
Alquanz ocis e li plusur neiet,
Mult grant eschec en unt si chevaler,

APPENDIX.

Li gentilz reis descendut est a piet,
Culchet sei a tere, si'n ad Deu graciet ; .
Quant il se drecet, li soleilz est culchet.
Dist l'emperere: 'Tens est del herberger;
En Rencesvals est tart del repairer :
Noz chevals sunt e las e ennuiez;
Tolez lur seles, les freins qu'il unt es chefs,
E par cez prez les laisez refreider.'
Respundent Franc : 'Sire, vos dites bien.' Aoi.

Li emperere ad prise sa herberge :
Franceis descendent en la tere deserte,
A lur chevals unt tolutes les seles,
Les freins ad or, e metent jus les testes ;
Liverent lur prez, asez i ad fresche herbe ;
D'altre cunreid ne lur poent plus faire.
Ki mult est las il se dort cuntre tere ;
Icele noit n'unt unkes escalguaite.

Li emperere s'est culcet en un pret;
Sun grant espiet met e sun chef li ber :
Icele noit ne s' volt il desarmer,
Si ad vestut sun blanc osberc saffret,
Laciet sun helme ki est ad or gemmet,
Ceinte Joiuse, unches ne fut sa per,
Ki cascun jur muet .xxx. clartez.
Asez avum de l' lance [oït] parler
Dunt Nostre Sire fut en la cruiz naffret :
Carles en ad l'amure, mercit Deu !
En l'oret punt l'ad faite manuverer.
Pur ceste honur e pur ceste bontet,
Li nums Joiuse [a] l'espee fut dunet :
Baruns franceis ne l' deivent ublier :
Enseigne en unt de Munjoie [ee]crier ;
Pur ço ne 's poet nule gent cuntrester.

Clere est la noit e la lune luisante ;
Carles se gist, mais doel ad de Rollant,
E de Oliver li peiset mult forment,
Des .xii. pers, e de la Franceise gent.
En Rencesvals ad laiset morz tanz genz!
Ne poet muer n'en plurt e ne s' desment,
E priet Deu qu'as anmes seit guarent.
Las est li reis, kar la peine est mult grant !
Endormiz est, ne pout mais en avant.
Par tuz les prez or se dorment li Franc.
N'i ad cheval ki puisset estre en estant :
Ki herbe voelt, il la prent en gisant ;
Mult ad apris ki bien conuist ahan !

Karles se dort cum hume traveillet ;
Seint Gabriel li ad Deus enveiet,
L'empereur li cumandet a guarder ;
Li angles est tute noit a sun chef,
Par avisiun li ad anunciet

G

D'une bataille ki encuntre lui ert;
Senefiance l'en demustrat mult gref:
Carles guardat amunt envers le ciel,
Veit les tuneires e les venz e les giels
E les orez, les merveillus tempez,
E fous e flambes i est apareillez:
Isnelement sur tute sa gent chet!
Ardent cez hanstes de fraisne e de pumer,
E cez escuz jesqu'as bucles d'or mier;
Fruisent cez hanstes de cez trenchanz espiez;
Cruissent osberes e cez helmes d'acer.
En grant dulor i veit ses chevalers:
Urs e leuparz les voelent puis manger,
Serpenz e guiveres, dragun e averser,
Grifuns i ad plus de trente millers!
Nen i ad cel as Franceis ne s'agiet,
E Franceis crient: 'Carlemagne, aïdez!'
Li reis en ad e dulur e pitet;
Aler i volt, mais il ad desturber:
De vers un gualt uns granz leons li vient,
Mult par ert pesmes e orguillus e fiers!
Sun cors meismes i asalt e requert;
Prenent sei a braz ambesdous por loitier,
Mais ço ne set quels abat ne quels chiet!
Li emperere ne s' est mie esveillet.

Apres icele li vient altre avisiun:
Qu'il ert en France, ad Ais, a un perrun,
En dous chaeines si teneit un brohun;
De vers Ardene veeit venir .xxx. urs,
Cascun parolet altresi cume [uns] hum;
Diseient li: 'Sire, rendez le nus!
Il nen est dreit que il seit mais od vos.
Nostre parent devum estre a sucurs.'
De sun paleis ez uns veltres acurt,
Entre les altres asaillit le greignur
Sur l'erbe verte, ultre ses cumpaignuns.
La vit li reis si merveillus estur!
Mais ço ne set li quels veint ne quels nun!
Li angles Deu ço ad mustret al barun.
Carles se dort tresqu'al demain cler jur.

12th CENTURY.

Le Roman de Rou.

Taillefer, qui mult bien cantoit,
sor un ceval qui tost aloit,
devant li duc aloit cantant
de Karlemaine et de Rollant
e d'Olivier e des vassals
ki morurent en Renchevals.
quant il ourent chevalcié tant

qu'as Englois vinrent aprismaut,
'sire,' dist Taillefer, 'merci,
jo vos ai longement servi,
tot mon servise me devés;
hui, s'il vos plaist, le me rendés.
por tot guerredon vos requier
et si vos voel forment proiier :
otroiiés moi, que jo n'i faille,
le premier colp de la bataille.'
li dus li a dit 'jo l'otroi.'
et Taillefer poinst a desroi,
devant tos les altres se mist.
un Englois feri, si l'ocist;
desos le pis par mi la pance
li fist passer oltre sa lance,
a terre estendu l'abati.
puis traist s'espee, altre en feri.
puis a crié 'venés, vénes!'
qui faites vos? ferés, ferés!'
dont l'ont Englois avironué
al secont colp qu'il out geté
et vos noise levee et cri,
et d'ambes pars puple estormi.
François al assaillir entendent
et li Englois bien se deffendent;
li un fierent, li altre botent.
tant sont hardi, ne s'entredotent.
es vos la bataille assemblee,
donc encore est grant renommee.
mult oissiés grant corneis
et de lances grant froisseis,
de machues grant fereis
et d'espees grant capleis.
a la fois Englois fuioient
et a la foie recovroient;
et cil d'oltremer assailloient
et bien sovent se retraioient.
Normant s'escrient 'dex aie,'
la gent engleske 'out out' s'escrie.
ço est l'enseigne que jo di
quant Englois salent hors a cri.
lors veissiés entre serjans
gelde d'Englois et de Normans,
grans barates et grans mellees,
bous de lances et cols d'espees.
quant Normans kiet, Engloie s'escrient,
de paroles se contralient
et mult sovent s'entredeffient,
mais ne sevent qu'il s'entredient.
cis vont avant, cist se retraient,
en mainte guise s'entrassaient,
hardi fierent, coart s'esmaient;
François dient qu'Englois abaient,

por la parole qu'il n'entendent.
cil empirent et cil amendent,
hardi fierent, coart gandissent,
com home font qui escremissent.
al assaillir François entendent
et li Englois bien se deffendent.
haubers percent et escus fendent,
grans cols reçoivent, grans cols rendent.

13th CENTURY.

Raous de Soisons.

Qant voi la glaie meure
Et le rosier espanir
Et sor la bele verdure
La rousee resplendir,
Lors souspir
Pour celi qui tant desir
Et aim, las, outre mesure.
Tout ausi coume larsure
Fait quanquele ataint bruir,
Fait mon vis taindre et palir
Sa douce regardeure
Qui el cors me vint ferir
Pour faire la mort sousfrir.

Molt fait douce bleceure
Boine amours en son venir,
Mais miex venroit la pointure
Dun escorpion sentir
Et morir
Que de ma dolor languir.
Elas, ma dame est si dure
Que de ma joie na cure
Na soi ne me veut tenir,
Si mocist a son plaisir;
Mais cest ades maventure
Kains dame ne poi servir
Ki le me vausist merir.

A, tres boine et desiree,
Onques dame ne fu si,
Se vous maves refusee
La joie dont je vous pri,
Enrici
Sont mi mortel anemi,
Et lor joie aves doublee
Et a moi la mort dounee.
Si ne lai pas deservi,
Conques nus hom ne transi
De mort si desesperee;
Mais bien veill estre peri
Puis que jai a vous fali.

He dieus, jou lai tant amee
Des ce que premiers la vi,
Conques puis dautre riens nee,
Nis de mon cuer ne goi,
Ains ma si
Laissie, pour amour de li
Que jou naim autre riens nee,
Mais quant ma dame houneree
Set quele a loial ami,
Bien devroit avoir merci
Se loiautes li agree;
Mais souvent avient ensi
Que ce sont li plus hai.

Cancounete, je tenvoi
A ma dame droitement,
Se li prie de par moi
Cor face tout son talent;
Car souvent
Vif plus dolereusement
Que cil qui mors fait estendre;
Mais sa douce face tendre
U toute biautes resplent,
Mart si le cors et esprent,
Que li carbons soz la cendre
Nart pas plus couvertement
Con fait li las qui atent.

14TH CENTURY.

JEHANS DE JOINVILLE.

Aprés ce que il fu croisié, se croisierent Robert le conte d'Artois, Auphons conte de Poitiers, Charles conte d'Anjou, qui puis fu roy de Cezile, touz troiz freres le roy; et se croisa Hugue duc de Bourgoingne, Guillaume conte de Flandres, frere le conte Guion de Flandres nouvellement mort; le bon Hue conte de Saint Pol, monseigneur Gauchier son neveu, qui moult bien se maintint outre mer et moult eust valu se il eust vescu. ei i furent le conte de la Marche et monseigneur Hugue le Brun son filz, le conte de Salebruche, monseigneur Gobert d'Apremont son frere, en qui compaingnie je, Jehan seigneur de Joinville, passames la mer en une nef que nous louames, pour ce que nous estione cousins; et passames de la a tout vint chevaliers; dont il estoit li disiesme et je moy disiesme.

A pasques, en l'an de grace qui le milliaire couroit par mil deux cenz quarante et huit, mandé je mes homes et mes fievez a Joinville, et la vegile de la dite pasque, que toute cele gent que je avoie mandé estoient venu, fu nez Jehan mon filz sire de Ancerville, de ma premiere femme qui fu seur le conte de Grantpré. toute cele semainne fumes en festes et en quarolles, que mon frere le sire de Vauquelour et les autres riches homes qui la estoient, donnerent a manger chascun l'un aprés l'autre, le lundi, le mardi, mecredi et le jeudi.

Je leur diz le vendredi ' seigneurs, je m'en voiz outre mer, et je ne soe se je revendré. or venez avant : se je vous ai de riens mesfait, je le vous desferai l'un par l'autre, si comme je ai acoustumé a touz ceulz qui vourront riens demander ne a moy ne a ma gent.' je leur desfiz par l'esgart de tout le commun de ma terre ; et pour ce que je n'eusse point d'emport, je me levoie du conseil et en ting quanque il raporterent, sanz debat.

Pour ce que je n'en vouloie porter nulz deniers a tort, je alé lessier a Mez en Lorreinne grant foison de ma terre en gage ; et sachiez que, au jour que je parti de nostre paiz pour aler en la terre sainte, je ne tenoie pas mil livrees de terre, car ma dame ma mere vivoit encore ; et si y alai moy disiesme de chevaliers et moy tiers de banieres. Et ces choses vous ramantevoiz je, pour ce que, se diex ne m'eust aidié, qui onques ne me failli, je l'eusse souffert a peinne par si lonc temps, comme par l'espace de six ans que je demourai en la terre sainte.

En ce point que je appareilloie pour mouvoir, Jehan sire d'Apremont et conte de Salebruche de par sa femme, envoia a moy et me manda que il avoit sa besoigne aree pour aler outre mer, il disiesme de chevaliers, et me manda que ce je vousisse que nous loissons une nef entre li et moy, et je li otriai : sa gent et la moie louerent une nef a Marseille.

15TH CENTURY.

CHARLES D'ORLEANS.

En regardant vers le pais de France,
ung jour m'avint, a Dovre sur la mer,
qu'il me souvint de la doulce plaisance
que souloye ou dit pais trouver.
si commençay de cueur a souspirer,
combien certes que grant bien me faisoit,
de veoir France que mon cueur amer doit.

Je m'avisay quo c'estoit nonsçavance
de telz souspirs dedens mon cueur garder ;
veu que je voy que la voye commence
de bonne paix qui tous biens peut donner.
pour ce tournay en confort mon penser :
mais non pourtant mon cueur ne se lassoit
de veoir France que mon cueur amer doi'.

Alors chargeay en la nef d'esperance
tous mes souhaitz, en les priant d'aler
oultre la mer sans faire demourance
et a France de me recommander.
or nous doint dieu bonne paix sans tarder
adonc auray loisir, mais qu'ainsi soit,
de veoir France que mon cueur amer doit.

Paix est tresor qu'on ne peut trop louer :
je he guerre, point ne la doy priser ;
destourbé m'a long temps, soit tort ou droit,
de veoir France que mon cueur amer doit.

EXAMINATION QUESTIONS.

1. What is meant by the Romance languages?
2. Explain the meaning of the terms: *langue d'oc* and *langue d'oïl*.
3. What was Raynouard's theory respecting the origin of the Romance languages, and by whom was this theory refuted?
4. Show that the Romance languages cannot be derived from classical Latin, but must be derived from the *lingua rustica* and the *media et infima Latinitas*. Explain these three terms.
5. Give the etymologies of *cheval, armée, jeu, parole, chat, tête*; and state to which kind of Latinity each etymon belongs.
6. Of what process of derivation are the following words examples: *soleil, sommeil, taureau*.
7. At what periods was the German element introduced into the vocabulary of the French language?
8. To what category belong the words introduced by the Norman invasion in the tenth century? Give examples.
9. To what category belong the words introduced by the German invasion in the fifth century? Give examples.
10. *Blanc, candide; bourgeois, citoyen; ouest, occident.* Give the etyma of these words, and remark thereon.
11. Explain the terms *synthetic* and *analytic*, as used with respect to language.
12. Mention the several characteristic processes in which the Romance languages agree among themselves, but differ from their Latin prototype.
13. How do you distinguish words of early formation (organic) and words of modern formation (inorganic, learned)?
14. *Acheter, accepter; chétif, captif; essaim, examen.* Give the etyma of these words and explain the twofold process of derivation in French.
15. Explain the main difference of French and Latin versification.
16. What is an accentuating language?
17. Give the etyma of *boutique, bourse, parole, moustache, migraine, serin*.
18. What is the main distinction between the inflections of Modern French and the *langue d'oïl*?
19. Mention the principal dialects of the *langue d'oïl*.
20. Mention some of the characteristic marks of the Norman dialect. Give examples.
21. Mention some of the characteristic marks of the Burgundian dialect.
22. What political causes were at work in giving the pre-eminence to the Norman and Burgundian dialects, and in finally producing a fusion of all the dialects?
23. *Roi, reine; poids, peser.* Explain the origin of these forms.
24. How far does etymology guide you in determining whether an *h* is aspirated or mute?
25. State, and exemplify the great law of the permutation of the mutes in the Romance languages.

26. In what positions are Latin consonants least subject to change?

27. Give the etymologies of *flairer, autel, orme, diacre;* and state the law according to which the liquids have been changed.

28. Explain the origin of the *u* in the following forms: *du, chevaux, Thibaut.*

29. Give examples of the intercalation of *d* between *n* and *r.*

30. Give examples of the intercalation of *b* between *m* and *r.*

31. In what class of the so-called irregular verbs does the intercalation of *d* between two liquids take regularly place in the future?

32. Exemplify the changes to which *t* in the middle of a word is subject.

33. Explain the origin of the circumflex accent in *âne, âpre.*

34. In *second* the *e* is pronounced like a *g*. What law of language has asserted itself in the spoken language, though not acknowledged in the written language?

35. Give examples of the change of initial *c* into *ch*. State the opinions of Diez and Burguy on this subject.

36. Explain every change of vowel and consonant in *coucher.*

37. Under what circumstances is a consonant most likely to suffer syncope?

38. Give the etyma of *raide, froid, lire, chatier, géant;* and remark on the change of the Latin middle consonant.

39. What phonetic change is undergone by Latin infinitives in —*ngere* (*cingere, fingere,* etc.)? In what French forms does the original Latin form reappear?

40. Give the etyma of *abeille, poivre, chèvre, savoir, cheveu;* and state the phonetic law according to which the consonant in the middle has been changed.

41. Why has the *p* in *vapeur, capitaine, stupide,* undergone no phonetic change?

42. Give the French derivatives of *corvus, vervex, varius.* Is the change of the Latin *v* in harmony with the general law of the permutation of consonants?

43. German (English) *w* undergoes what change in passing into French? Give the French words for *war, Walter, wicket.*

44. What do we mean by saying that a vowel is long by Romance position?

45. What is meant by *diphthongaison?*

46. When does the *diphthongaison* of *a* regularly take place?

47. What change does *u* undergo before simple consonants, excepting *m* and *n?* Give examples.

48. Is the *i* in *mais, faine,* owing to *diphthongaison?*

49. *Moi, trois, roi; bien, tient, vient.* Account for the difference of the phonetic change of the Latin *e.*

50. Give examples of long Latin *i* remaining unchanged.

51. Give examples of the *diphthongaison* of short *i* into *oi* and *ei.*

52. Give the etyma of *langue, dans, sanglot.*

53. Give the meanings and etymologies of *poison, potion; dauer, doter; porche, portique;* and remark on the double forms of the French derivative.

54. Give the French derivatives of *locare, laudare; falx, falsus; novus, novem.*

QUESTIONS.

55. *Son*, sound; *son*, his; *le palais*, palace; *le palais*, palate. Explain the identity of form and difference in meaning.

56. Account for the difference of gender in *le somme* and *la somme; le livre* and *la livre*.

57. Give a few phrases in which the French definite article has preserved the force of a demonstrative pronoun.

58. Explain the meaning and origin of *ès* in *bachelier ès lettres, ès mains*.

59. Explain the forms *du, au, des, aux*.

60. Give an account of the Old French declension, and especially of what has been called *la règle de l's*.

61. *Garçon, baron, felon* are originally what case? What are their respective nominative forms?

62. Remark on the following expressions: *Hôtel-Dieu, Château-Thierry, de par le Roi*.

63. Prove that French substantives derived from Latin substantives must be derived from the accusative form.

64. Account for the final *t* in *nuit*; and the final *n* in *mon, ton, son, rien*.

65. Of what gender are the names of trees and shrubs in Latin and French respectively? To what cause is this change of gender to be attributed?

66. Why are *courage* and *voyage* of the masculine gender, but *rage, image, plage*, feminine?

67. Account for the respective genders of *oratoire, purgatoire, écritoire, corpuscule, formule*.

68. Latin substantives in —*or* are in French either masculine or feminine. Give the rule.

69. What was the probable cause which determined the change of gender of Latin abstracts in —*or*?

70. Distinguish between *le pendule* and *la pendule, le vapeur* and *la vapeur, un trompette* and *une trompette, le mémoire* and *la mémoire, un aide* and *une aide, un office* and *une office*.

71. Account for the difference in gender and meaning of *le critique*, and *la critique, le satire* and *la satire, le poste* and *la poste, le parallèle* and *la parallèle*.

72. Give the French derivatives, with their respective genders, of *alnus, ulna, liber, libra, somnus, summa, palmus, palma*.

73. What is the etymology of *bonheur* and *malheur?* Show that the popular etymology (*bona hora, mala hora*) is erroneous.

74. How is the feminine gender of *la patente, la constituante, la sécante* to be accounted for?

75. What is the gender of substantives which are originally French past participles?

76. Form nomina agentis from *blanchir, fournir, polir, courir, couvrir*.

77. Mention the only abstract noun in *eur* which retains its original Latin gender.

78. Substantives ending in —*ance* are derived from ——? and those ending in —*ence* from ——?

79. Give a historical account of the suffix —*erie*, and compare the same with the German suffix —*erei*.

80. What is the gender of substantives derived from adjectives?

81. Are the suffixes —*ard* and —*aud* of Latin origin?

82. What explanations have been given of the suffixes *at, et, ot*?

83. In Old French we read: des ordres *royale*, des lettres *royale*. Why not *royales*?

84. *Grand' mère, grand'rue.* Show that the apostrophe had its origin in the ignorance of grammarians.

85. State the reason why the masculine plural of many adjectives in —*al* is at present doubtful.

86. What remnants are there in Modern French of the Latin comparison of adjectives?

87. *Moderne, ancien, souverain.* Of what rare process of the derivation of adjectives are these words examples? Give some similar derivations in Latin.

88. From what language were the adjectival suffixes —*esque*, —*asque*, imported. What Greek and German suffixes correspond to —*esque, asque*?

89. *Les quinze-vingts, six vingts.* Of what method of counting are these expressions remnants?

90. Give the etyma of *en, dont, beaucoup, maint, y.*

91. *Me, moi; te, toi; se, soi.* Explain the origin of these double forms.

92. *Leur* is derived from ———? Give analogous derivations in Latin.

93. What is the meaning of *ma mie*? How should these words be properly spelled?

94. Give the etymologies of *celui, celle, ce, cette.*

95. *Si l'on* . . . Why is the *l'* put in here? What part of speech is it?

96. How are the Latin Passive Voice and the Deponent Verb replaced in French?

97. What is the origin of the suffix of the future tense: aimer—*ai, as, a,* etc.?

98. Explain the suffix of the conditional: aimer—*ais, ais, ait,* etc.

99. Account for the final *s* in *je vends, je vendais*. At what time does this *s* first appear in the written language?

100. *A-t-il, aime-t-il.* Of what is this *t* a remnant? Why has it been preserved only in the interrogative form?

101. *Il parloit, il parlait; anglois, anglais.* Give an account of these two modes of spelling.

102. In which forms of the verbs *tenir* and *venir* does *diphthongaison* take place? Explain the causes of this process.

103. Give the two etymologies of *être*, and show which is the correct one.

104. Analyse the form *j'aurai*.

105. Which two Latin forms have coalesced in the French participle present?

106. What is the origin of the adverbial suffix—*ment*.

107. Give the etymologies of: *depuis, dans, avant, parmi, selon, avec, devant, hormis.*

108. Give the names of the seven days of the week, with their etymologies.

109. Give a few compound substantives formed by the combination of an imperative with a substantive.

110. Give a few compound substantives formed by the combination of an adjective and a substantive.

OPINIONS OF THE PRESS.

From the " Revue Critique."

On ne peut que donner des éloges à la manière dont M. Meissner a compris et exécuté son travail : la disposition est commode, la forme claire et élégante. Je louerai particulièrement ce qui concerne la *dérivation* des noms, des adjectifs et des verbes, les observations intéressantes sur le genre des substantifs, les études disseminées à plusieurs endroits sur les *doubles formes* et les *homonymes*, le petit chapitre sur la composition. M. Meissner fait rentrer à l'occasion les faits qu'il rencontre en français dans l'ensemble des phénomènes généraux des langues indo-européennes ; c'est une bonne méthode et qu'il a souvent heureusement employée, qui d'autres fois aurait demandé à être appliquée avec plus de prudence. . . . . Nous souhaitons donc à son petit livre tout le succès qu'il mérite : il répandra sans doute en Angleterre l'étude historique de notre langue.—GASTON PARIS.

From the " Revue de l'Instruction Publique."

Si, de l'autre côté de la Manche, les grammaires et les guides-ânes pour apprendre notre langue ne font pas défaut, il n'existait pas, que je sache, d'ouvrage sérieux sur l'histoire de notre langue. Le livre de M. Meissner vient à propos combler cette lacune ; il est court, clair, et puisé aux meilleures sources. L'auteur a eu l'heureuse idée d'y joindre en appendice quelques fragments d'ancien français. . . . . Nous voyons avec satisfaction l'histoire et la grammaire scientifique de notre langue désormais représentées dans la littérature scolaire de l'Angleterre par ce recommandable manuel.—H. GAIDOZ.

From the " Athenæum."

The Professor of Modern Languages in the Queen's University presents in this text-book the groundwork of his lectures in Queen's College, Belfast, and a good solid foundation it is, on which both lecturers and students may build with safety. Of course it is not, nor is it intended to be, light reading. The author's object is not to exhibit the results of modern philology in an attractive form for popular readers, but rather to supply materials of thought and suggestive hints to those who wish to acquire a philological knowledge of the French language in its successive stages. . . . . Beginning with a brief but excellent account of the origin of modern French—including an accurate survey of the several characteristic distinctions between the Romance languages and the parent Latin, and a description of the three dialects of the Langue d'Oïl—he proceeds to set forth under the head of "Phonology" the various changes of letters which have taken place in passing from one period to another. The remainder of the work is devoted to "Morphology," or an account of the formation of words by the modification or addition of syllables or the composition of words. The forms assumed by verbs at different periods of the language are clearly and fully set forth. By way of illustration the etymology of many words is explained—of some more than once, because they happen to be instances of more than one general principle—which is no bad thing, and is far better than giving derivations in an isolated way without pointing out the law to which they conform.

From the "Spectator."

This work is emphatically a book for students, or rather for teachers.

From the "Educational Times."

A well-written and thoughtful treatise on the history and philology of the French language, scholarly in its tone and treatment, and full of valuable information on many of the most interesting points of comparative grammar. Though primarily intended for advanced students following a course of college lectures or preparing for some of the higher competitive examinations, it may be used with great advantage in the upper forms of our public schools.

From the "Museum."

This book supplies a want which has long been felt. The French language is at present learned too much as a mere matter of rote, and the pupil knows nothing of the formation and history of the language. Dr. Meissner's work supplies this information in a satisfactory manner. It is scholarly, accurate, and thorough. The author traces the various inflections up to their original forms, and goes minutely into the changes which words have undergone in passing from Latin and other languages into French. It is a work which ought to be used in all schools where Latin is taught, and it will be read with much interest and much profit alike by those who teach French and those who teach Latin. The book has only to be known to come into extensive use.

ImTheStory.com

Personalized Classic Books in many genre's

Unique gift for kids, partners, friends, colleagues

Customize:
- Character Names
- Upload your own front/back cover images (optional)
- Inscribe a personal message/dedication on the inside page (optional)

Customize many titles Including
- Alice in Wonderland
- Romeo and Juliet
- The Wizard of Oz
- A Christmas Carol
- Dracula
- Dr. Jekyll & Mr. Hyde
- And more...

WS - #0051 - 040324 - C0 - 229/152/9 - PB - 9781313796859 - Gloss Lamination